C000111495

The LEADING LADY

By
GERALDINE BONNER

AUTHOR OF

*To-morrow's Tangle, The Pioneer,
Rich Men's Children, The
Book of Evelyn*

INDIANAPOLIS
THE BOBBS-MERRILL COMPANY
PUBLISHERS

COPYRIGHT, 1926
BY THE BOBBS-MERRILL COMPANY

Printed in the United States of America

PRINTED AND BOUND
BY BRAUNWORTH & CO., INC.
BROOKLYN, NEW YORK

THE LEADING LADY

The
LEADING LADY

PROLOGUE

ONE of the morning trains that tap the little towns along the Sound ran into the Grand Central Depot. It was very hot in the lower levels of the station and the passengers, few in number— for it was midsummer and people were going out of town, not coming in—filed stragglingly up the long platform to the exit. One of them was a girl, fair and young, with those distinctive attributes of good looks and style that drew men's eyes to her face and women's to her clothes.

People watched her as she followed the porter carrying her suit-case, noting the lithe grace of her movements, her delicate slimness, the froth of blonde hair that curled out under the brim of her hat. She appeared oblivious to the interest she aroused and this indifference had once been nat-

ural, for to be looked at and admired had been her
normal right and become a stale experience. Now
it was assumed, an armor under which she sought
protection, hid herself from morbid curiosity and
eagerly observing eyes. To be pointed out as
Sybil Saunders, the actress, was a very different
thing from being pointed out as Sybil Saunders,
the fianceé of James Dallas of the Dallas-Parkinson case.

The Dallas-Parkinson case had been a sensation
three months back. James Dallas, a well-known
actor, had killed Homer Parkinson during a quarrel in a man's club, struck him on the head with a
brass candlestick, and fled before the horrified
onlookers could collect their senses. Dallas, a
man of excellent character, had had many friends
who claimed mitigating circumstances—Parkinson, drunk and brutal, had provoked the assault.
But the Parkinson clan, new-rich oil people,
breathing vengeance, had risen to the cause of
their kinsman, poured out money in an effort to
bring the fugitive to justice, and offered a re-

ward of ten thousand dollars for his arrest. Of course Sybil Saunders had figured in the investigation, she was the betrothed of the murderer, their marriage had been at hand. She had gone through hours of questioning, relentless grilling, and had steadily maintained her ignorance of Dallas' whereabouts; from the night of his disappearance she had heard nothing from him and knew nothing of him. The Parkinsons did not believe her statement, the police were uncertain.

As she walked toward the exit she carried a newspaper in her hand. Other people in the train had left theirs in their seats, but she, after a glance at the head-lines, had folded hers and laid it in her lap. Three seats behind her on the opposite side of the aisle she had noticed a man—had met his eyes as her own swept back carelessly over the car—and it was then that she had laid the paper down and looked out of the window. Under the light film of rouge on her cheeks a natural color had arisen. She had known he would be there but was startled to find him so close.

Now as she moved across the shining spaciousness of the lower-level waiting-room she stole a quick glance backward. He was following, mounting the incline. It was the man who had gone up with her on Friday. She had been out of town several times lately on week-end visits and one of them was always on the train. Sometimes it was a new one but she had become familiar with the type.

She knew he was behind her at the taxi stand as she gave the address in a loud voice. But he probably would disappear now; in the city they generally let her alone. It was only when she left town that they were always on hand, keeping their eye on her, ready to follow if she should try to slip away.

The taxi rolled out into the sweltering heat; incandescent streets roaring under the blinding glare of the sun. Her destination was the office of Stroud & Walberg, theatrical managers, and here in his opulent office set in aerial heights above the sweating city, Mr. Walberg offered

her a friendly hand and a chair. Mr. Walberg, a
kindly Hebrew, was kindlier than ever to this particular visitor. He was sorry for her—as who in
his profession was not—and wanted to help her
along and here was his proposition:

A committee of ladies, a high-society bunch
summering up in Maine, wanted to give a play for
charity. They'd got the chance to do something
out of the ordinary, for Thomas N. Driscoll, the
spool-cotton magnate who was in California, had
offered them his place up there—Gull Island was
the name—for an outdoor performance. Mr.
Walberg, who had never seen it, enlarged on its
attractions as if he had been trying to make a
sale—a whole island, just off the mainland, mag-
nificent mansion to be turned over to the company, housekeeper installed. The crowning touch
was an open-air amphitheater, old Roman effect,
tiers of stone seats, said to be one of the most
artistic things of its kind in the country. The
ladies had wanted a classic which Mr. Walberg
opined was all right seeing the show was for char-

ity, and people could stand being bored for a
worthy object. *Twelfth Night* was the play they
had selected, and as that kind of stage called for
no scenery one thing would go as well as another.

The ladies had placed the matter in Mr. Walberg's hands, and he had at once thought of Sybil
Saunders for Viola. She had played the part
through the provinces, made a hit and was in his
opinion the ideal person. There was a persuasive,
almost coaxing quality in his manner, not his
usual manner with rising young actresses. But,
as has been said, he was a kindly man, and had
heard that Sybil Saunders was knocked out,
couldn't get the heart to work; also, as she was a
young person of irreproachable character, he inferred she must be hard up. That brought him
to compensation—not so munificent, but then
Miss Saunders was not yet in the star class—and
all expenses would be covered, including a week at
Gull Island. This opportunity to dwell in the
seats of the mighty, free of cost, with sea air and
scenery thrown in, Mr. Walberg held before her
as the final temptation.

He had no need for further persuasion for Miss Saunders accepted at once. She was grateful to him and said so and looked as if she meant it. He felt the elation of a good work done for the charitable ladies—they could get no one as capable as Sybil Saunders for the price—and for the girl herself whose best hope was to get back into harness. So, in a glow of mutual satisfaction, they walked to the door, Mr. Walberg telling over such members of the cast as had already been engaged: Sylvanus Grey for the Duke, Isabel Cornell for Maria, John Gordon Trevor for Sir Toby—no one could beat him, had the old English tradition—and Anne Tracy for Olivia. At that name Miss Saunders had exclaimed in evident pleasure. Anne Tracy would be perfect, and it would be so lovely having her, they were such friends. Mr. Walberg nodded urbanely as if encouraging the friendships of young actresses was his dearest wish, and at the door put the coping stone on these agreeable announcements:

"And I'm going to give you my best director,

Hugh Bassett. If with you and him they don't pull off a success the Maine public's dumber than I thought."

Later in the day he saw his director and told him of Miss Saunders' engagement.

"Poor little thing," he said. "She looks like one of those vegetables they grow in the dark to keep 'em white. But it'll be the saving of her. Now you go ahead and get this started—three weeks rehearsal here and one up there ought to do you. And keep me informed—if any of these swell dames turn up asking questions, I want to know where I'm at."

Her business accomplished, Miss Saunders went home. She lived in one of those mid-town blocks of old brownstone houses divided into flats. The flats were of the variety known as "push button" and "walk up," but she pushed no button as she knew hers would be tenantless. Letting herself in with a latchkey she ascended the two flights at a rapid run, unlocked her door and entered upon the hot empty quietude of her own domain.

The blinds in the parlor were lowered as she had left them. She pulled one up with a nervous jerk, threw her hat on a chair, and falling upon the divan opened the paper that she had carried since she left the Grand Central Station.

The news of the day evidently had no interest for her. She folded the 'pages back at the personal column and settled over it, bent, motionless, her eyes traveling down its length. Suddenly they stopped, focussed on a paragraph. She rose and with swift, tiptoe tread went into the hall and tried the front door. Coming back she took a pad and pencil from the desk, drew a small table up to the divan, spread the newspaper on it, and copied the paragraph on to the pad. It ran as follows:

"Sister Carrie:
Edmund stoney broke but Albert able to help him. Think we ought to chip in. Can a date be arranged for discussing his affairs?
                    Sam and Lewis."

She studied it for some time, the pencil suspended. Then it descended, crossing out letter after letter, till three words remained—"Edmunton, Alberta, Canada." The signature she guessed as the name he went by.

She burned the written paper, grinding it to powder in the ash-tray. The newspaper she threw into the waste-basket where Luella, the mulatto woman who "did up" for her, would find it in the morning. She felt certain Luella was paid to watch her, that the woman had a pass-key to the mail-box and every torn scrap of letter or note was foraged for and handed on. But she had continued to keep the evil-eyed creature, fearful that her dismissal would make them more than ever wary, strengthen their suspicion that Sybil Saunders was in communication with her lover.

The deadly danger of it was cold at her heart as she lay back on the divan and closed her eyes. Through her shut lids she saw the paragraph with the words of the address standing out like the writing on the wall. She had heard directly from him once, a letter the day after he had fled; the only one that even he, reckless in his despair, had dared to send. In that he had told her to watch the personal column in a certain paper and had given her the names by which she could identify the paragraphs. She had watched and twice found the veiled message and twice waited in sickening fear for discovery. It had not happened. Now he had grown bolder, telling her where he was—it was as if his hand beckoned her to come. She could write to him at last, do it this evening and take it out after dark. Lying very still, her hands clasped behind her head, she ran over in her mind letter-boxes, post-offices where she might mail it. Were the ones in crowded districts or those in secluded byways, the safest? It was like walking through grasses where live wires were hidden.

A ring at the bell made her leap to her feet with wild visions of detectives. But it was only Anne Tracy, come in to see if she was back from her visit on the Sound. It was a comfort to see Anne, she always acted as if things were just as they had been and never asked disturbing questions. In the wilting heat she looked cool and fresh, her dress of yellow linen, her straw hat encircled by a wreath of nasturtiums had the dainty neatness that always marked Anne's clothes and Anne herself. She was pale-skinned and black-haired, satin-smooth hair drawn back from her forehead and rolled up from the nape of her neck in an ebony curve. Because her eyebrows slanted upward at the ends and her eyes were long and liquid-dark and her nose had the slightest retroussé tilt, people said she looked like a Helleu etching. And other people, who were more old-fashioned and did not know what a Helleu etching was, said she looked like a lady.

She was Sybil's best friend, was to have been her bridesmaid. But she knew no more of Sybil's secrets since Jim Dallas had disappeared than any one else. And she never sought to know—that was why the friendship held.

They had a great deal to talk about, but chiefly the *Twelfth Night* affair. Anne was immensely pleased that Sybil had agreed to play. She did not say this—she avoided any allusions to Sybil's recent conducting of her life—but her enthusiasm about it all was irresistible. It warmed the sad-eyed girl into interest; the Viola costume was brought from its cupboard, the golden wig tried on. When Anne took her departure late in the day, after iced tea and layer cake in the kitchenette, she felt much relieved about her friend— she was "coming back," coming alive again, and this performance off in the country, far from her old associations, was just the way for her to start.

Anne occupied another little flat on another of the mid-town streets in another of the brownstone houses. Hers was one room larger, for her brother, Joe Tracy, lived with her when not pursuing his profession on the road. There were hiatuses in Joe's pursuit during which he inhabited a small bedroom in the rear and caused Ann a great deal of worry and expense. Joe apparently did not worry, certainly not about the expense. Absence of work wore on his temper not because Anne had to carry the flat alone, but because he had no spending money.

They said it was his temper that stood in his way. Something did, for he was an excellent actor with that power of transforming himself into an empty receptacle to be filled by the character he portrayed. But directors who had had experience of him, talked about his "natural meanness" and shook their heads. When his name was mentioned it had become the fashion to add a follow-up sentence: "Seems impossible the same parents could have produced him and Anne." People who tried to be sympathetic with Anne about him got little satisfaction. All the most persistent ever extracted was an admission that Joe was "difficult." No one—not even Sybil or Hugh Bassett—ever heard what she felt about the fight he had had with another boy over a game of pool which had nearly landed him in the Elmira Reformatory. Bassett had dragged him out of that, and Bassett had found him work afterward, and Bassett had boosted and helped and lectured

him since. And not for love of Joe, for in his
heart Bassett thought him a pretty hopeless
proposition.

That evening, alone in her parlor, Anne was
thinking about him. He had no engagement and
no expectation of one, and it was not wise to leave
him alone in the flat without occupation. "Satan"
and "the idle hands" was a proverb that came to
your mind in connection with Joe. She went to
the window and leaned out. The air rose from the
street, breathless and dead, the heated exhalation
of walls and pavements baked all day by the mer-
ciless sun. Passers-by moved languidly with a
sound of dragging feet. At areaways red-faced
women sat limp in loose clothing, and from open
windows came the crying of tired little children.
To leave Joe to this while she was basking in the
delights of Gull Island—apart from anything he
might do—it wasn't fair. And then suddenly the
expression of her face changed and she drew in
from the window—Hugh Bassett was coming
down the street.

The bell rang, she pushed the button and pres-

ently he was at the door saying he was passing
and thought he'd drop in for a minute. He was a
big thick-set man with a quiet reposeful quality
unshaken even by the heat. It was difficult to
think of Bassett shaken by any exterior accident
of life, so suggestive was his whole make-up of a
sustained equilibrium, a balanced adjustment of
mental and physical forces. He had dropped in a
great deal this summer and as the droppings-in
became more frequent Anne's outside engagements
became less. They always simulated a mutual
surprise, giving them time to get over that some-
what breathless moment of meeting. .

They achieved it rather better than usual
to-night for their minds were full of the same subject. Bassett had come to impart the good news
about Sybil, and Anne had seen her and heard all
about it. There was a great deal of talking to be
done that was impersonal and during which one
forgot to be self-conscious. Finally when they
had threshed out all the matters of first importance Bassett said:

"Did you tell her that Walberg wanted Aleck Stokes for the Duke?"

"No, I didn't say a word about it. What was the use? It would only have upset her and you'd put a stop to it."

"You can always be relied on, Anne, to do the tactful thing. Walberg was set on it. Stokes can't be beaten in that part and he's at liberty. But I wasn't going to take any chances of her refusing, and if Stokes was in the company I was afraid she might."

"I don't know whether she'd have gone that far, but it would have spoiled everything for her and for the rest of us too. It's all plain sailing now except for one thing"—she stopped and then in answer to his questioning look—"about the police. If they have her under surveillance, as people say, what'll they do about it up there?"

The big man shrugged:

"Camp in the village on the mainland—they certainly can't come on the island. We've special instructions about it—no one but the company to be allowed there till the performance. Did she speak to you about that?"

"No, she hardly ever alludes to the subject. But they *would* keep a watch on her, wouldn't they?"

He nodded, frowning a little at a complication new in his experience:

"I should think so—a woman in her position. Men under sentence of death have been unable to keep away from the girl they were in love with. And then she may know where he is, be in communication with him."

"Oh, I don't think that," Anne breathed in alarm. "She'd never take such a risk."

"Well, we're her friends and we're as much in the dark as anybody. I only know one thing—if they try to hound her down on that island—the first chance she's had to recuperate and rest— I'll—"

A slight grating noise came from the hall. Anne held up a quick cautioning hand.

"Take care," she murmured. "Here's Joe."

Joe came in, his Panama hat low on his brow. He gave no sign of greeting till he saw Bassett, then he emitted an abrupt "Hello" and snatched off the hat:

"Little Anne's got a caller. Howdy, Bassett! How's things?"

There was a jovial note in his voice, a wide grin of greeting on his face. It was evident the sight of Bassett pleased him, and he stood teetering back and forth on his toes and heels, looking ingratiatingly at the visitor. He was like Anne, the same delicate features, the same long eyebrows and the same trick of raising them till they curved high on his forehead. But his face had an elfish, almost malign quality lacking in hers, and the brown eyes, brilliant and hard, were set too close to his nose. He was two years younger than she—twenty-two—but looked older, immeasurably older, in the baser worldly knowledge which had already set its stamp upon him.

He launched forth with a suggestion of pouncing eagerness on the *Twelfth Night* performance.

He had heard this and that, and Anne had told
him the other. His interest surprised Anne, he
hadn't shown much to her; only a few laconic
questions. And she was wondering what was in
his mind, as she so often wondered when Joe held
the floor, when a question enlightened her:

"Have you got anybody to play Sebastian
yet?"

"No. I wanted that boy who played with her
on the southern tour last year, but he's in England. He gave a first-rate performance and he
did look like her."

"That was a lucky chance. You'll search the
whole profession before you get any one that
looks like Sybil's twin brother."

"He ought to bear some resemblance to her,"
and Bassett quoted, " 'One face, one voice, one
habit, and two persons.' I wonder if Shakespeare
had twins in his eye when he wrote the play."

"Not he! They did the same in his day as they
do now—dressed 'em up alike and let it go at that.
Why, Mrs. Gawtrey, the English actress, when

she was over here, had a boy to play Sebastian
who looked as much like her—well, not as much as
I look like Sybil."

Bassett had seen his object as Anne had and
was considering. He had been looking forward
to the week at Gull Island with Anne, it loomed in
his imagination as a festival. There would be a
pleasant, companionable group of people,
friendly, working well together. But Joe among
them——

The boy, looking down at his feet, said slowly:

"What's the matter with letting me do it?"

"Nothing's the matter. I've no doubt you
could, but you and she have about as much resemblance as chalk and cheese."

Joe wheeled and gathering his coat neatly
about his waist walked across the room with a
mincing imitation of Sybil's gait. It was so well
done that Bassett could not contain his laughter.
Encouraged, the boy assumed a combative attitude, his face aflame with startled anger, and
striking out, at imaginary opponents, shouted:

" 'Why there's for thee, and there and there and there. Are all the people mad?' " Then as suddenly melted to a lover's tone and looking ardently at Anne said: " 'If it be thus to dream then let me sleep.' "

"Oh, he *could* play it," she exclaimed, and Bassett weakened before the pleading in her eyes.

He understood how to manage Joe, he could keep him in order. The boy was afraid of him anyway, and by this time knew that his future lay pretty well in Bassett's hands. If there was anything Anne wanted that was within his gift there could be no question about its being hers.

She was very sweet, murmuring her thanks as she went with him to the door and assurances that Joe would acquit himself well. Bassett hardly heard what she said, looking into her dark eyes, feeling the soft farewell pressure of her hand.

Joe had left the sitting-room when she went back there and she supposed he had gone to bed. But presently he came in, his hat on again and said he was going out. She was surprised, it was past eleven, but he swung about looking for his cane, saying it was too hot to sleep. She tried to detain him with remarks about the new work. He answered shortly as was his wont with her, treating it as a small matter, nothing to get excited about—also a familiar pose. But she noticed under his nonchalance a repressed satisfaction, the glow of an inner elation in his eyes.

THE performance was over and the audience
was dispersing. Gull Island, colored to a chromo
brightness by the declining sun, had not showed
so animated an aspect since the reception for the
Spanish ambassador last July. People-in pale-
tinted summer clothes were trailing across from
the open-air theater and massing in a group as
gay as a flower garden at the dock. Some of
them had gone into the house, taken the chance to
have a look at it—when the Driscolls were "in res-
idence" you couldn't so much as put your foot on
the rocks round the shore. Others lingered, having a farewell word with the actors, congratulat-
ing them—it was the right thing to do and they
deserved it. The committee was very affable,
shaking hands with Mr. Bassett the director and
Miss Saunders the star, who, in her page's dress

34

with the paint still on her face, looked tired, poor girl, but was so sweet and unassuming.

It had been a complete success. The matrons who had organized it scanned the crowd converging toward the dock and smiled the comfortable smile of accomplishment. The summer home for tenement children could build its new wing and employ that man from Boston who had such modern scientific methods. And the matrons, stiff in the back and unbecomingly flushed after sitting two hours in the sun on the stone seats of the theater, drew toward one another on the wharf and agreed that everything had gone off beautifully and the board should at once write to Mr. Driscoll and thank him for lending the island.

The fleet of boats, rocking gently on the narrow channel that separated Gull Island from the mainland, took on their freight and darted off. They started in groups then broke apart. Speed boats that had come from points afar, whizzed away with a seething rush and a crumple of crystal foam at the bow. The launches skimmed, light-winged, the white flurry of their wakes like threads that stretched back to the island.

People turned and looked at it—sun-gilded in an encircling girdle of Prussian blue sea. The rocks about its base, the headlands that rose above, were dyed to an orange red and against this brilliancy of primary colors the pines stood out darkly silhouetted. On the rise above the wharf the long brown structure of the house spread, rambling and irregular, built, it was said, to suggest an outgrowth of the rocky foundation. The watchers could see in the open place beyond the side balcony the actors standing motionless, spaced in a group. Yes, having their photographs taken; there was the camera man who'd been taking pictures during the performance. And they craned their necks for a last look at the lovely scene and the picturesque assemblage of players.

Part of the flotilla carried the Hayworth villagers—all-year residents of the little town on the mainland. Some of the more solid citizens were

in the launch that old Gabriel Harvey owned,
which had been used by the actors in their week's
stay. Hayworth had gathered a great deal of
information about these spectacular visitors,
some from Gabriel and some from Sara Pinkney
who was Mr. Driscoll's housekeeper, living in
Hayworth all winter and in summer reigning in
the Gull Island kitchen. Mr. Driscoll had wired
Sara to go over and open up and take charge
while they were there—spare nothing, those were
his orders. And Sara had done it, not wanting to,
but apart from its being Mr. Driscoll's wishes
which she had followed for the last ten years, she
had felt it her duty to keep an eye on the prop-
erty. Every day she came over to Hayworth for
supplies and had to appease the local curiosity,
which she did grudgingly, feeling her power.

Now at last the Hayworth people had had a
first-hand view of the actors—the whole company, dressed up and performing—and they
fitted Sara Pinkney's description to them. Olivia,
that was Miss Tracy, the one she said was so re-

fined and pleasant-spoken. And the Duke was Alexander Stokes. He was the feller that had come after the others because the first man took sick—wonderful the way he did it considering, didn't miss a word. And the woman who stood round and "tended on" Olivia was his wife. Sara hadn't said much about her. Well, she wasn't of much importance anyhow or she'd have had more acting to do. But that boy who was Viola's twin, he was Miss Tracy's brother, and Sara had said he and Miss Saunders didn't get on well, *she* could see it though they didn't say much. And here piped up the butcher's wife who was more interested in the play than in personalities:

"I don't see how Olivia took him for the page she was in love with. He didn't look like Viola in the face. She was real pretty, but he'd a queer sly mug on him, that boy."

"Aw, you can't be too particular. You don't need to have it so real."

"I guess she was meant to be blinded by love. And him dressed the same, hair and all, might lead her astray."

"I don't see how you could have 'em look just alike unless they'd get an actress who had a real twin brother, and maybe you'd go the whole country over and not find that."

"He ain't like her no way," growled old Gabriel from the wheel, "I seen 'em both when they wasn't acting and he's an ugly pup, that one."

Then the boat grating on the Hayworth wharf, Gabriel urged them off. He hadn't got through yet, got to go back for part of the company who were calculating to get the main line at Spencer, and after that back again for the Tracy boy. He muttered on as they climbed out, grumbling to himself, which nobody noticed as it had been his mode of expression for the last thirty years.

The swaying throng of boats emptied their cargoes and the thick-pressed crowd, moving to the end of the wharf, separated into streams and groups. Farewells, last commending comments, rose on the limpid sea-scented air. Everybody was a little tired. The villagers, dragging their feet, passed along the board walks to their vine-draped piazzas. They would find their kitchens hot and dull that night after two hours in the enchanted land of Illyria. The waiting line of motors absorbed the summer visitors, wheeled off and purred away past the white cottages under the New England elms. The matrons sank gratefully upon the yielding cushions, rolling by the dusty buggies, the battered Fords, the lines of bicycle riders, into the quiet serene country where the shadows were lying long and clear. Yes, it had been a great success; from first to last there hadn't been a hitch.

II

THAT was how the audience saw it, but they were outsiders. There was one outsider left on the island, Wally Shine, the photographer sent by the Universal Syndicate to take pictures of what was a "notable society event" in a place of which the public had heard much and seen nothing. He had arrived that morning with two cameras and a delighted appreciation of the beauty he was to record. But, unlike the other outsiders, his impressions extending over a longer period had not been so agreeable. He had seen the actors at close range, in their habits as they lived, lunched with them, watched the last rehearsal, taken a lot of pictures of Miss Saunders in the house and garden. And he had sensed an electric disturbance in the atmosphere, and come upon evidences of internal discord.

41

That was at the last rehearsal, when the poetic Viola had lost her temper like an ordinary woman and jumped on the Tracy boy—something about the place he stood in—nothing, as far as Shine could see, to get mad about. And the boy had answered in kind like the spitting of an angry cat. An ugly scene that the director had to stop.

Then the man Stokes who played the Duke, a handsome, romantic-looking chap—something was the matter with him. "Eating him" was the phrase Shine used to himself and it wasn't a bad one. He had a haunted sort of look, as if his mind was disturbed, especially when he'd turn his eyes on Miss Saunders. Shine had noticed him particularly when they gathered for the group pictures; his hands were unsteady and the perspiration was out on his forehead though the air was cool from the sea. His wife—the woman they called Flora—was on to him. Shine saw her watching him, sidelong from under her eyelids, the way you watch a person when you don't want them to see it.

The photographer was a fat easy-going man, inured to the vagaries of those who follow the arts. But he was sensitive to emotional stress and he felt it here—below the surface—and was moved to curiosity.

The photographs were finished and the group broke up. Part of the company were going and they ran toward the house—a medieval route—the big Sir Toby with a rolling amble, Sir Andrew, long and lank, cavorting like a mettlesome steed. Their antic shadows fled before them over the dried sea grass, and their voices, shouting absurdities, rang rich and deep-throated on the crystal atmosphere.

Miss Saunders and Miss Tracy linked arms and moved off toward the head-lands. Receding in the amber light they were like a picture from some antique romance—the noble lady and her page. One in narrow casings of crimson brocade, the other in short swinging kilt and braided jacket of more sober gray. Shine, fascinated, watched them pacing slowly over the burnished grass.

Flocks of sea-gulls, roused by their voices, rose
into the air, poised and wheeled, one moment dark,
the next floating shapes of gold. He turned to go
and saw that Stokes was watching them too, intent like a hungry dog, the hand that held a stalk
of feathered grass against his lips, trembling.

The photographer shouldered his camera and
went toward the house. A jeweled brightness of
garden extended along its seaward front. Beyond
this was the one stretch of cultivated turf on the
island, an emerald slope leading to the cuplike hollow that held the amphitheater. He skirted the
side balcony, the wide-flung doors giving a
glimpse of an entrance hall, and turning the corner emerged upon the land front of the long ca-
pacious building. The surroundings on this side
had been left as nature made them—rock shelves
and ledges, devoid of vegetation, a path winding
round them from the entrance to the wharf. Hayworth showed across the channel in a clustering of
gray roofs from which smoke skeins rose straight
into the suave rose-washed sky. The water

rushed between, a swollen tide, threads of white dimpled eddies, telling of its racing speed.

The door on this side of the house opened directly into the living-room. No hall within or porch without interfered with the view; the path ended unceremoniously at the foot of two broad steps that led to the threshold. On the lower of these steps Shine found a lady sitting smoking a cigarette. This was the Maria of the cast, Mrs. Cornell in private life. She was still in her costume, her redundant figure swelling over the traditional laced bodice, the rouge on her cheeks hardly showing against the coat of sunburn a week at Gull Island had laid on. He had found her as easy as himself, good-humoredly loquacious and not involved in the prevailing discord. An admirable person to clear up mysteries. He sank down beside her on the step and took the cigarette box she flipped toward him.

"Wouldn't you think," she said, "a man as rich as this Mr. Driscoll would fix up round here better?"

Shine, who had artistic responses, had long
learned not to intrude them on the uninitiated.

"I guess he liked it wild," he suggested, and lit
a cigarette.

"But it looks so rough, not a flower bed or a
vase—just paths. That one there," she pointed
to a path that skirted the side of the house and
dipped to a small grove of pines below, "goes
through those pines and up to that summer-house.
Nothing on the way and what's the summer-house
when you get there? Old style rustic work with
vines. You'd suppose he'd build a temple and
have some marble benches round. The way the
rich spend their money always gets me."

Shine had been in the grove of pines, a growth
of stunted trees filling in a hollow. He had followed the path through it, up the slope to the
summer-house and beyond to where the bluff
dropped away in a sheer cliff to the channel.
They called the place "The Point" as it projected
beyond the shore line in a rocky outthrust shoulder, gulls circling about it, water seething below.

He looked there now, let his glance slip along the
curve of headlands till it reached the two girls,
perched on a boulder like a pair of bright-plum-
aged birds. He was thinking how to approach the
matter in his mind, when Mrs. Cornell went on:

"I don't see what any one wanted to build a
house here for—cut off this way. It's too lone-
some. With the tide at the full as it is now you
can't get ashore without a motor-boat. You know
that current's something fierce."

He looked down at it, its rushing corded surface purple dark:

"Looks to be some current."

"It would carry you out and 'Good night' to
you. Gabriel who runs the launch told me. Set's
right out to sea someway. And the rise and fall
to it—I couldn't tell you how many feet it is, but
you'll see for yourself to-night if you're awake—
all the channel bare, nothing but rocks and mud.
And across the middle of it to Hayworth, a
causeway. That's the only way you can get
ashore at *low* tide. High or low you're pretty

well marooned. It's seclusion all right if that's what you're after."

Shine was after information and with the talk running on tides and causeways he saw no chance of getting it. So he tried to divert the garrulous lady:

"That's Miss Saunders and Miss Tracy out there looking at the sunset."

Mrs. Cornell answered with emphasis:

"Yes, *they're* friends."

"Aren't you all?"

"Some of us knew each other before we came here," was her cryptic reply. Then she added pensively: "Six months ago you'd never have found Sybil Saunders looking at a sunset. She was the *brightest* thing!"

"Awful misfortune that what happened to her."

She gave a derisive sound at the inadequacy of the word:

"Hah—awful! Took the heart right out of her. If you ever saw a girl in love it was she— bound up in him. Everything ready, the wedding day set, the trousseau made." Tears rose in her eyes and she dove into her tight bodice for a handkerchief. "Never to be worn, Mr. Shine—that's life."

Shine gave forth sympathetic murmurs and Mrs. Cornell, dabbing at her eyes, furnished data between the dabs:

"Two men drinking too much and then a fight, and before anybody knew, murder! If there hadn't been a brass candlestick near Jim Dallas' hand it would never have happened. Honest to God, Mr. Shine, there was nothing evil in that young man. But the Parkinson family are camped on his trail. The evil's in them, if you ask me, with their rewards and detectives."

"I wonder if she knows where he is."

"I guess there's more than one wondering that," the lady murmured.

"Terribly hard position for her if she does know—or if she doesn't."

Shine looked at the page's figure on the rock. She carried the thing stamped on her face. He had noticed it particularly where he had taken the photographs of her in the living-room. They were time exposures with his small camera, attempts to catch her fragile prettiness in artistic combinations of light and shade. Once or twice the mask had been dropped and he had seen the drooping lines, the weariness, and something like fear on the delicate features.

For a space they smoked in silence. Round the corner of the house the tall figure of Stokes strolled into view. He looked at the seated girls, then turned and glanced behind him with a quick and furtive sweep of the eyes. At the sight of them he nodded, walked down to the wharf and dropped on a bench.

Shine lowered his voice:

"What's the matter with him?"

Mrs. Cornell met his eyes; her own were narrowed and sharp.

"What makes you think anything is?"

"His whole make-up—something's wearing on him."

She blew out a long shoot of smoke and, watching it, murmured:

"Yes, it's out on him like a rash. He oughtn't to have come, but the first man they had, Sylvanus Grey, took sick and Mr. Walberg engaged Stokes in a hurry and sent him up. It's spoiled everything for the rest of us. He's crazy about Sybil if you want to know what's the matter with him."

"Oh!" It came with an understanding inflection, the haggard glances rising on Shine's memory.

"Can't hide it, doesn't want to hide it. There's no shame in him, tracking after the girl. And it's not as if he got any encouragement. She can't bear him; that's why she has Anne Tracy out there, afraid if she sits alone five minutes he'll come loping up. You'd think if he didn't have any pride he'd have some feeling for his wife. She's half crazy with jealousy, burning up with it. These purple passions are all right in books, Mr. Shine, but believe me they're not comfortable to live with."

"I felt it."

"I guess you would, it's in the air. All of us cooped up in this place where you can't get off. I thought it was going to be such a nice restful change. But lord! It's about as restful as camping on the side of Vesuvius. Sybil and Joe Tracy ready to fight at the drop of the hat and Flora going round in circles and Stokes like one of those fireworks that starts sputtering and you don't know whether they're going to explode or die on you. I tell you I'll be glad when we get out of here to-morrow morning."

There was a footfall in the room behind them and Mrs. Cornell turned to see who was coming.

"Oh, Flora," she said. "Come out and take a look at the sunset. It's something grand."

The woman stepped out and stood beside them. She had changed her costume and her narrow blue linen dress outlined her too slender figure. Shine thought she would have been pretty if she had not looked so worn and thin. He noticed the brightness of her dark eyes, brilliant and quick-moving

as a bird's. There was red on her cheek-bones, a
flushed patch that was not rouge. Mrs. Cornell's
expression recurred to him, "burning up"—the
meager body, the hot high color, the dry lips resolutely smiling, suggested inner fires.

"Yes," she answered, "it's a wonderful
evening."

"Take a cig." Mrs. Cornell offered the box.

"Sit down, there's plenty of room." Shine
moved up.

"No, I can't sit down. There's something about
the air that makes you restless—too stimulating
maybe." She raised her voice and called to her
husband, "Aleck, aren't you coming in to change
your clothes?"

Without moving the man called back:

"Not yet. There's no hurry."

She turned to Shine with a little condoning air
of wifely tolerance:

"Mr. Stokes has been shut up so long in town
he can't get enough of the fresh air."

"He's enjoying the scenery, too," Shine answered, and saw her eyes travel to the two figures on the rock.

"Oh, that of course—that's the best part of it." Then in a tone of bright discovery: "Why look where Anne and Sybil are! Have they been there long?"

"Ever since I've been here." Mrs. Cornell's voice was more than soothing, bluffly reassuring as the voice of one who tells a child there is no ghost. "And ever since Mr. Shine got through the pictures! Wallowing in the beauties of nature like the rest of us."

"Won't you wallow, too?" Shine indicated the long unoccupied space on the step.

She shook her head:

"I like moving about. Something in this place gets on my nerves, it's like being in a jail." On a deep breath she shot out, "I hate it," and stepped back into the room.

"Going?" Mrs. Cornell veered round to follow her retreating figure.

"Yes. I enjoy the scenery better when it hasn't got people in it."

They looked at each other; a still minute of eye communication.

"She's all worked up," he murmured.

Her answer was to point to the two girls and then to Stokes:

"Now she'll keep her eye on them from somewhere else—probably the side piazza. That's the way you are when you're jealous— the sight of it kills you and you can't stop watching."

"Lord!" whispered Shine into whose life no such gnawing passions had entered. And he thought of the girl in the page's dress who was afraid to sit alone, and the man on the wharf brooding within sight of her, and the woman who was hovering round them like a helpless distracted bird.

III

THE launch was on its way back for those of
the actors who were leaving. Gabriel, squatting
by the engine, calculated the distribution of his
time. After he'd taken them across he'd have his
supper and then go back for Joe Tracy, who was
leaving on the seven fifteen for his vacation.
When Joe was disposed of, Gabriel was to meet
two Boston sports who had engaged him for a
week's deep-sea fishing at White Beach, twenty-
five miles down the coast. It was a strenuous
program for the old man and he grumbled to himself about it, the grumbling gaining zest by antici-
pations that some of them would be late. If it
was any of the actors, by gum, he wouldn't wait
for them, with the sports ready to take him along
in their car at seven. By the time he drew near
the island he had grumbled himself into a state of

irascible defiance against any one who would dare upset his plans.

To warn them of his coming he sounded the whistle and its shrill toot acted like a magic summons. A group of men, bearing suit-cases and bags, emerged from the entrance and ran down the path, Bassett following. Miss Pinkney's helper, a native of Hayworth, hurried from the kitchen wing, a suit-case in her hand, and even the august Sara herself appeared in the doorway of her domain.

Gabriel quieted down—they were all ready and waiting—and then saw Joe Tracy come round the corner of the house in his Sebastian dress. The old man muttered profanely—why wasn't the d——d cub getting ready? And as the boat made its landing, he called out:

"Say, you'd better be gettin' them togs off. I'll be back here for you at a quarter to seven."

The boy, leaping lightly from rock to rock, grinned without answering. The picturesque dress suited him, he looked almost handsome, and

with the feathered cap on his golden wig set rak-
ishly aslant, he moved downward with a taunting
debonair swagger. Gabriel didn't like him anyway and now his impudent face, framed by the
drooping blond curls, looked to the launch man
malignantly spiteful.

Gabriel could say no more then for the confusion of good-bys possessed the wharf. The
actors shouted them out even to Miss. Pinkney,
flattering assurances of their inability to forget
her and her cooking. She waved a condescending
hand and permitted herself a smile, for she was
very glad to get rid of them.

But Gabriel wasn't going to go till he'd made
things clear. He appealed to Bassett whom he
had privately sized up as the only one of the outfit who was like the rational human males of his
experience. Besides he had seen that Joe Tracy
respected, if not feared, the director:

"I'll be back here at quarter to seven for the
Tracy boy, and I'm tellin' him he's got to be
ready. I can't waste no time settin' round waitin'
and if he's not here on the dot—"

"That's all right," Bassett put a comforting hand on his shoulder and turned to Joe. "You heard that, Joe?"

The boy answered with his sneering grin:

"What's got the old geezer? Does he think I'm as deaf as he is?"

Gabriel's weather-beaten visage reddened. He was not in the habit of being called an "old geezer" and he was not deaf. But the actors, all in the boat, were clamoring to start. They had a train to make—get in ancient servitor, and turn on the current. Miss Pinkney's helper, with her hat on one side and her face crimson, giggled hysterically, and in a chorus of farewells the boat chugged off.

The three men left on the wharf went up the path to the doorway where Shine and Mrs. Cornell had resumed their seats. Shine was struck by their difference of type,—if you went the world over you couldn't find three more varied specimens. The only one he liked was Bassett, something square and solid about him and a good straight look in his eyes. The kind of chap, Shine thought, you'd ask directions of in the street and who'd give 'em to you no matter what hurry he was in. And he'd a lot of authority—the way he managed this wild-eyed bunch showed that. Shine had noticed, too, a sort of exuberant quality of good will about him—like a light within shining out—and set it down to relief at having got through without any one blowing the lid off.

They stopped at the steps and Joe Tracy made his good-bys. He was going camping in the woods with his friend Jimmy Travers, who was to meet him at Bangor to-night. They'd stay there twenty-four hours getting their stuff together, then be off for the northern solitudes—no beaten tracks for them. He left, jauntily swinging his kilted skirts, a whistled tune on his lips. Soon after, Stokes departed, saying he was going to change his clothes. His air was nonchalant, lounging up the steps and crossing the living-room with a lazy padding stride.

A door to the right opened into the entrance

hall. Here he and his wife occupied a ground-floor room. It was on the garden front of the house opposite the stairway that led to the second story. He listened at the panel before he entered, then softly turned the knob, and, inside, as softly closed the door. Shut in and alone his languid pose fell from him like a cloak. An avid eagerness sharpened his features and directed his hands, pulling open his valise and taking from it a small leather case. Moving back from the window he pushed up his sleeve, took the hypodermic from the case and pressed in the needle. When he had restored the bag to its place, he threw himself on the bed and lay with closed eyes feeling the ineffable comfort, grateful as an influx of life, vitalize and soothe his tortured being.

Mrs. Cornell and Shine rose up and followed him. Mrs. Cornell had her packing to get through and wanted Miss Pinkney's help. Shine was going to see if the pantry would do for a dark room, intending to take some flashlight photographs of the company that evening. He had found in a cabinet all the flashlight requisites and thought it would be an interesting memento of their visit—each of them to have a picture.

"They've got everything here," he said as he pointed to the corner where he had made his find. "Not alone all the supplies, but two first-class cameras and a projector. I suppose some of the family took it up for a fad."

Mrs. Cornell opined it was to occupy the young men. There were several Driscoll boys and if you didn't give them something to do they'd get into mischief. Though, if you asked her, she didn't see any chances for mischief in *this* jumping-off place, unless the high tide washed in a few mermaids.

Then they passed on through the left doorway, into the side wing of the house. Here Shine, who was domiciled in the butler's bedroom, disappeared into the adjoining pantry and Mrs. Cornell trod resolutely on into the kitchen, being one of the few members of the company who was not afraid of the housekeeper.

Miss Pinkney, who was sitting upright in a stiff-backed chair, rose respectfully. She was a lean slab-sided woman of fifty, with tight-drawn hair and a long horse face. She had disapproved bitterly of the intrusion of the actors upon the sacred precincts of Gull Island and though she had been rigidly polite hoped that her disapproval had got across. Anyway, she had had the satisfaction of putting cotton sheets on their beds and serving their meals on the kitchen china. If they did any damage to the house or premises she was ready to assert her authority, and she had been on the watch. But they had been careful and orderly and treated her with the proper deference, and in her heart the revolutionary thought had arisen that they were equally considerate and more amusing than the usual run of Gull Island guests. Also they gave her a subject of conversation that would last out the winter.

Mrs. Cornell broached her request and Miss Pinkney agreed. She was even very pleasant about it, showing a brisk friendly alacrity—with the helper gone there'd only be a cold supper and she could dish that up in two shakes. Together they left the kitchen and on the stairs Mrs. Cornell hooked her plump arm inside Miss Pinkney's bony one and said when Mr. Shine took the flashlights that night he must take one of them as the "feeder" and the other as the "fed."

IV.

BASSETT had gone into the house too. As he
crossed the living-room he noticed its deserted
quietude, in contrast to the noise and bustle that
had possessed it an hour ago.

It was a rich friendly room, comfortably home-
like in spite of its size, for it crossed the center of
the house, its rear door opening on the garden as
the one opposite did on the path. It was spacious
in height as well as width, its walls rising two
stories. Midway up a gallery ran, on three sides
of which the bedrooms opened. The fourth side,
on the seaward front, was flanked by a line of
windows, great squares of unsullied glass that
looked over the garden and the amphitheater to
the uplands and the open ocean. There were
tables here, raking wicker chairs, and low settees
with brilliant cushions, books lying about and

65

smokers' materials. In the room below the character of a hunting lodge had been suggested by mounted deer heads, Indian blankets, baskets of cunning weave and animal skins on the floor. But it was an idealized hunting lodge, with seats in which the body sank luxuriously, and softly shaded lights. Round the deep-mouthed chimney the scent of wood fires lingered, the fires of birch logs that leaped there when Gull Island lay under storm and mist. The architect had not diminished the effect of size and unencumbered space by stairs. The second story was reached by two flights, one in the entrance hall, one in the kitchen wing.

Bassett opened the door into the hall where again all was quiet, none of the jarring accents that occasionally rose from the Stokes' room. He walked across the gleaming parquette to the library which he had used for his office. There were no signs of the hunting lodge here—a scholarly retreat, book-lined, with leather armchairs and lights arranged for readers' eyes, a place for delightful hours if one had time to drowse and poke about on the shelves. Two long French windows framed a view of the channel and Hayworth dreaming among its elms. He went to one of the windows and looked out. The girls were still sitting there, and, as he looked at them, an expression of infinite tenderness lay like a light on his face. It was the light Shine had noticed, allowed to break through clearly now that no one was there to see.

He sat down at the desk; there were letters for him to answer, addenda of the performance to check up. He moved the papers, looked at them, pushed them away, and, resting his forehead on his hands, relinquished himself to a deep pervading happiness. Yesterday Anne had promised to marry him.

His mind, held all day to his work, now flew to her—memories of her face with the down-bent lids as he had asked her, and the look in her eyes as they met his. Brave beautiful eyes with her soul in them. It had been no light acceptance for her,

it meant the surrendering of her whole being, her
life given over to him. He heard her voice again,
and his face sank into his hands, his heart trembling in the passion of its dedication to her service.
Anne, whom he had coveted and yearned for and
thought so far beyond his reach—his! He would
be worthy of her, and he would take such care of
her, gird her round with his two arms, a buckler
against every ill that life might bring. She'd had
such a hard time of it, struggling up by herself
with Joe hung round her neck like a millstone.

At the memory of Joe he came to earth with a
jarring impact. He dropped his hands and
stared at the papers, his brows bent in harassed
thought. Joe had broken the charm, obstructed
the way to the paradise of dreams like the angel
with the flaming sword—though angel was not
exactly the word. Bassett had heard something
that morning from Sybil which must be looked
into—something he could hardly believe. But
Joe being what he was you never could tell. It
had been a mistake to bring him, with Sybil a
bunch of nerves and Stokes shunted unexpectedly

into their midst. And now he felt responsible, he'd have it out with Joe before he left. One more disagreeable scene before they separated to-morrow, and Bassett, like Mrs. Cornell, felt he'd thank Providence when they were all on the train in the morning. Meantime he'd go over his papers while he waited for the boy who had gone to his room to dress. The door was open and he could hear him as he came down the stairs.

· Anne was approaching the house, a slender crimson figure, her hair in the sunset light shining like black lacquer. She was smiling to herself—everything was so beautiful, not only Gull Island and this hour of tranquil glory, but the mere fact of existing. Then she saw Flora Stokes sitting on the balcony and realized that in this golden world there were people to whom life was a dark and troublous affair. She wanted to comfort Flora, let some of the happiness in her own heart spill over into that burdened one. But she knew no way of doing it, could only smile at the haggard face the woman lifted from her book.

"Oh, Mrs. Stokes, reading," she cried as she

ran up the steps. "How can you read on such an evening as this?"

Flora Stokes said she had been walking about till she was tired, and then glanced at the distant rock:

"You've left Sybil out there."

There was no comfort or consolation that could penetrate Mrs. Stokes' obsession. Anne could only reassure:

"She's coming in soon. She just wanted to see the end of the sunset."

She passed into the hall, sorry—oh, so sorry! But the library door was open and she halted, poised birdlike for one glance. The man at the desk had his back to her and she said nothing, yet he turned, gave a smothered sound and jumped up. She shut her eyes as she felt his arms go about her and his kisses on her hair, her senses blurred in a strange ineffably sweet confusion of timidity and delight.

"Oh, Anne," she heard his voice between the kisses. "I was waiting for you."

"Some one will see us," she whispered. "Take care."

She could feel the beating of his heart through his coat. Her hands went up to his shoulders feeling along the rough tweed and with her lids down-drooped she lifted her face.

"Darling," he breathed, when the kiss was over, "I thought you were never coming."

"I had to stay with Sybil. She didn't want to be alone."

"But *you* wanted to be here?"

"Just *here*," she laid a finger on his breast and broke into smothered, breathless laughter.

He laughed too and they drew apart, their hands sliding together and interlocking. It was all so new, so bewilderingly entrancing, that they did not know how to express it, the man staring wonder-struck, the girl, with her quivering laugh-ter that was close to tears, looking this way and that, not knowing where to look.

"I ought to go," she whispered. "They'll be coming," but made no move.

"Wait till they do." Then with a sudden practical facing of realities, "When will we be married?"

"Oh, not for ages! I'm not used to being engaged yet!"

"I am—I never was before but I must have had a talent for it, I've taken to it so well."

"Oh, Hugh!" Her laughter came more naturally, his with it. They were like a pair of children, delighting in a little secret. "Won't they be surprised when they hear? Nobody has a suspicion of it."

She looked so enchanting with her eyebrows arched in mischievous query that he made a movement to clasp her again, and then came the creak of an opening door from the floor above.

"Hist!" she held up a warning hand and slid away, her face, glancing back for a last look, beautiful in its radiant joy.

Bassett moved to the stair-foot. Once again he had to come down to earth with a bump. He passed his hand over his face as if to wipe off an

expression incompatible with disagreeable inter-
views. This must be Joe.

It *was* Joe, dressed for travel in knickerbockers
and a Norfolk jacket, a golf cap on the back of
his head. He carried an overcoat across his arm,
in his hands a suit-case and a fishing rod done up
in a canvas case. At the sight of Bassett he
halted, and the elder man noticed a change in his
expression, a quick focusing to attention.

"Oh," he said. "Want to see me, Bassett?"

"Yes, I want to speak to you before you go."

Joe descended. Stopping a step above Bassett,
he set down his baggage and leaned on the banister, politely waiting.

Bassett spoke with lowered voice:

"I heard something this morning that I can
hardly believe—an accusation against you. That
you've been using your position here to act as one
of the police spies who've been keeping tab on
Sybil."

The boy looked at him with impenetrable eyes
and answered in the same lowered key:

"Who told you that?"

"She did. She accuses you of having come here with that intention, got the job knowing that no outsiders were to be allowed on the island."

Bassett was certain he had paled under his tan, but his face retained a masklike passivity.

"Sounds as if she might be losing her mind."

"You deny it?"

The boy gave a scornful shrug:

"Of course I deny it. I shouldn't think it would be necessary to ask that. She's had a down on me for some time—everybody's seen it, snapping and snarling at me for nothing—and I suppose she wants to get an excuse for it."

"She says she came upon you examining a letter of hers, holding it up to the light. And three days ago she found you in her room looking over the papers in her desk."

"Ah!" he made a gesture of angry contempt. "It would make a person sick—examining her letters! I was looking through the mail bag to see if there was anything for me. If I took up one of hers by mistake does that prove I was examining it?"

"How about the other thing?"

"Being in her room? Yes, I was there. I went in to get a stamp. I had an important letter to go when Gabriel took over the mail and it was time for him. All the rest òf you were out. Her room was next to mine and I went in. I never thought anything about it, no more than I would have thought about going into Anne's or yours or anybody else's. She's nutty, I tell you. You can't trust her word. And if she says I'm hired to spy oñ her she's a damned——"

He stopped. Basset's eye was steady on him in a cold command he knew. There was the same cold quality in the director's voice:

"If the position Sybil's in has made her suspicious, that's all right. I'd like to believe it was the case. But if any of us—supposedly her friends—had inserted themselves in here to carry on police surveillance, using *me* to get them in— well, I'd not think *that* all right."

Joe leaned over the banister. His control was shaken, his voice hoarsely urgent:

"You got to be fair, Bassett, and because you're sorry for her is no reason to set her word over mine. It's *not* true. Don't you believe me?"

Bassett did not answer for a moment. He wanted to believe and he doubted; he thought of Joe's desire to come, of the reward:

"I guess you know, Joe, you can trust me to be fair, but I'm not going to commit myself till I know. It won't be hard to do that. I can find out when I get back to New York. And take this from me—if what Sybil says is true I'm done with you. No more help from me, no more work in any company I manage. And I fancy the whole theatrical profession will feel the same way." He drew back from the stair-foot. The disagreeable interview was over. "There's no good talking any more about it. Accusations and denials don't get us anywhere. We'll let it rest till I've made my inquiries. I'll say good-by now and hope you'll have a good time in the woods."

He turned and walked up the hall to his room on the garden front next the Stokes'. Joe gathered his luggage and went the opposite way, down the hall and into the big central apartment. He stepped with gingerly softness as if he were creeping away from something he feared might follow him. At the entrance door he set down his luggage and as he bent over it a whispered stream of curses flowed from his lips. He cursed Bassett and his luck, but Sybil with a savage variety of epithet and choice of misfortune, for she had undone him. Straightening up he looked blankly about—his inner turmoil was such he hardly knew where he was—and he retraced his steps, seeking the seclusion of his room, went up the stairs in noiseless vaulting strides like a frightened spider climbing to its web.

V

ANNE had taken off her costume and slipped into a negligée to do her packing comfortably, and then decided she had better bid good-by to Joe first. Bidding good-by was not an obligation between them, but she had to get the key of his trunk—it was going back to New York with hers—and her heart in its new warmth yearned to him, her only relation. She wanted to tell him her great secret, see an answering joy leap into his face, for he thought more of Bassett than anybody, and he'd be so surprised to hear that Anne, her charms held at a low valuation, had won such a prize.

Her room was the first on the left side of the gallery, Joe's next to Sybil's on the land front of the house. She passed the long line of closed doors, voices coming from behind Mrs. Cornell's,

78

and reaching Joe's, knocked. A "Come in," un-
invitingly loud and harsh, answered her and she
entered. Joe was sitting in a low armchair, bent
forward, his hands holding a cane with which he
was tapping on the floor. The bright square of
the window was behind him, framing rosy sky and
the green shore-line. He looked up to see who it
was; then, without greeting or comment, drooped
his head and went on lightly striking the cane on
the carpet as if he were hammering in a nail and
it required all his attention. Anne felt dashed,
his manner might have been the same to an intrud-
ing stranger. She asked about the key, and he
nodded to the bureau where it lay. The trunk
was packed and locked? To that he gave an as-
senting grunt, then raised his head and looked at
her—what have you come here for, the look said.

It was not a reception to encourage confidences
and she stood uncomfortably regarding him, trying to find something to say that would dispell
his somber ill humor.

"You're all ready? Where's your luggage?"

"Down by the door. Is there anything else you want to know?"

"*I* don't want to know, I was thinking of you. You're always late, and it's different here with only one way to get ashore and Gabriel never willing to wait."

He made no answer, continuing his play with the cane. · She knew that something was wrong and sat down on the arm of a chair, uneasy, wondering what it was:

"I'm glad you've managed this holiday. And it's so jolly having Jimmy Travers, he's such a sport. You'll meet him to-night at Bangor. At the Algonquin Inn—wasn't that the name of it?"

"Um."

"I want to be sure because if any important mail should come for you I could send it there to meet you on your way back. Algonquin Inn—I'll remember that. Then off to-morrow morning— it'll be lovely in the woods now."

"Any place would be lovely after this beastly hole."

"Beastly hole! I thought you liked it!"

"Did you? Take another guess."

"You expected to like it. You wanted to come."

He made no answer, but slanting his body side-wise with an air of ostentatious endurance, took out his watch and looked at it. She ignored the hint—you couldn't be sensitive with Joe—and leaning toward him asked:

"What's the matter, Joe?"

"Matter—with what?"

"You! Has anything happened?"

"Oh, no, nothing's happened." His words were mincingly soft. "What *could* happen with such a charming lot of people and Miss Saunders play-ing the star rôle in the performance and out."

It was Sybil then—he'd been working himself into a bad temper over her treatment of him. Anne had thought it odd he had not mentioned it before:

"You're angry with Sybil, and I don't think she has been very nice to you. I've noticed it, especially the last three days and this afternoon when we were sitting out there on the rock I tried to make her tell me why."

He raised his head; the profile sharply defined against the window showed a working muscle in the cheek: "And did she tell you?"

"No, she didn't seem to want to talk about it. She changed the subject."

"How considerate!"

"There's no sense getting annoyed about it because I don't think she has any reason. You have to make excuses for her. She's gone through this awful experience and her nerves are all wracked to pieces. You have to be patient and take her as a sort of afflicted person—"

He dashed the cane down and jumped to his feet in a volcanic explosion of rage:

"I don't take her that way. I take her for what she is, a damned lying hypocrite."

"Joe!" She was amazed, not so much at the words, as at the suddenness of the outburst and the contorted passion of his face.

"She thinks she can treat me any way she wants
and get away with it. Well, she'll find her mistake, she's taken the wrong turning this time.
She takes me for a yellow dog she can kick whenever she feels like it. But I got teeth, I can bite.
Patient—be patient— God, I'd like to wring her
neck, the damned——."

He used an epithet that brought Anne to her
feet, breathing battle: "Don't dare to say that
of my friend, Joe Tracy."

He stood in front of her, hump-shouldered, with
outthrust jaw, brows drawn low over eyes gleaming like a cat's. She had never seen him look like
that; he seemed a stranger, a horrible stranger,
and she drew away, aghast at the revelation of a
being so sinisterly unfamiliar. Her look brought
him back to self-control. He jerked his head up,
ran a hand over his hair, and turned away to the
window. Standing there he said:

"Well, I take that back. I didn't mean to say
it. But she's made me mad; I think she'd make
anybody."

The tone, surly still, had a placating quality; it was as near an apology as Joe could ever come. She felt immeasurably relieved for he had frightened her. To see the family cat, whose vagaries of temperament she knew by heart, suddenly transformed into a tiger, had given her a shock. She accepted his amends without comment, but she could not resist a sisterly admonition:

"If you'd only stop getting mad over small things you'd find life so much easier."

He laughed:

"Good advice from little sister! It doesn't cost anything and it's the correct *ingenue* pose."

He turned from the window smiling, Joe at his most amiable. If he had met her this way she would have poured out her secret. But her high mood had fallen and besides he wanted her to go— he said he had a letter to write yet. Lounging toward her he put his hands on her shoulders, gave her a light kiss on the cheek and pushed her toward the door.

On her way back along the gallery she recalled

his face in that moment of rage with troubled question. She wondered if there was more disturbing him than she knew—it was an extraordinary exhibition of anger for such a cause. Also she had not felt sure that his change of mood was genuine, his laugh had rung false, and when he had laid his hands on her shoulders she had felt their coldness through the thin stuff of her negligée. She heaved a sigh of relief at the thought that he was going. In his present mood there was no knowing what clashes there might be, and it was the last evening, and there would be a full moon, and she and Bassett would walk like lovers under its magic light.

When her door had closed, the gallery and living-room became as quiet as though the house were unoccupied. Sybil, approaching it, heard no sound of voices, a fact that reassured her, for the long day had tired her and she had no mind for talk. She was coming in by the balcony when she saw Flora Stokes sitting there reading and deflected her course toward the path that skirted

the building's front. If Flora noticed her she
made no sign, her eyes glued to her book, and
Sybil, stepping softly, for she dreaded the woman's resentful glances, passed along to the entrance of the living-room. The place was deserted and she stopped on the threshold for a last
look at the sky's fading splendors.

Across the depths of the room the door into the
hall opened, but so gently that she did not hear it.
Stokes made this noiseless entrance in the hope
that she might be there, and now, seeing his hope
fulfilled, closed the door as carefully, standing
against it watching her.

If the conventional garb of the street was not
as becoming to his darkly Byronic style as the
trappings of the Duke, he was still unusually
handsome. A figure of distinction in its lean
grace, with proud hawk features and the deep-set
melancholy eyes that the matinée girl loves. Even
his pallor had charm in their opinion, adding to
his romantic suggestion. Gull Island sun and
breezes had left no trace upon it; his face against

the background of the door was a yellowish white.

Seeing that she did not turn he pronounced her name. At that she wheeled, lightning-quick, and came forward from beneath the deep jut of the gallery assuming as unconcerned a manner as she could.

"Lovely evening," she said as she advanced. "It's been hard to come in."

"Evidently from the length of time you stayed out there. I've been waiting for you."

It was not a propitious beginning, especially as he still stood against the door as if intending to bar her exit.

"I'm going up-stairs to dress now."

"There's plenty of time. You can give me a few minutes. I've something I want to say to you."

"Oh, Aleck!" She stopped with an air of weary expostulation. *"Don't* say anything more. *Don't* begin that dreadful subject. I'm sick of it, I loathe it and *can't* you see it isn't any use?"

He went on as if he hadn't heard her:

"I've been trying for days, ever since I came here. And you keep avoiding me, always having some one with you. Now we'll be going to-morrow, we may not have another chance, and I must see you and tell you"—he stopped and looked at the gallery. "Did I hear a step up there?"

She had heard nothing and thought it odd that he should be so suddenly cautious. Discretion had been the last quality he had heretofore shown.

"I *have* avoided you and I'm going to continue doing it. Please move away from the door. It's silly to stand in front of it for I can go round by the garden, but I'm tired and I don't want to."

He came forward, speaking as he advanced.

"This isn't what you think. I'm done with that. You've made me understand, you've got it across, Sybil. I'm not going to bother you any more with that subject you loathe and think so dreadful. But I can't help loving you and wanting to help you." She gave an exasperated gesture and made a move to pass him. As she did so, he said: "I've heard something of Jim Dallas."

She stopped as if all animating force had been stricken out of her, a "What?" expelled on a caught breath.

"Just before I left town I met an actor who says he saw him."

"Are you telling me the truth?"

"Why should I lie? What do I gain by it? I swore the fellow to secrecy and came up here to tell you and I've been trying——"

She broke in: "Was he sure? Where was it?"

The change in her manner would have crushed the hope in any man. Shunning him like a leper, she now drew close and laid her hand on his arm.

"I can't tell you here. It's too dangerous, too many people coming and going."

"It *was* Jim?"

"It *was*. It's quite a story, more than just seeing him. But we've got to get somewhere away from all these damned doors——"

One of them opened—that into the hall behind them. They heard it and wheeled round, faces sharp-set in defensive interrogation. It was

Flora Stokes. She rested on the threshold look-ing at them, and Stokes, his senses more alert than the girl's, withdrew his arm from her clasp.

"Oh, Flora," he said, his voice supremely light and easy. "Were you looking for me?"

Mrs. Stokes said no, she had come to put her book back. She walked slowly to a table and placed her book on the corner. The room was very still as she did this. Stokes, his hands deep in his pockets, moved his head, following her prog-ress as if it roused his curiosity. The girl stood without a sound, the scene passing under her eyes with a mirage-like unreality.

"It seems I've intruded," said Mrs. Stokes, each syllable meticulously clear and precise. "But if you want to be alone I should think you'd have chosen another place."

"Having chosen this is a pretty good proof we didn't want to be alone," retorted her husband.

She gave a light jeering sound of disbelief and walked to the entrance. On the sill she turned and looked at them with smoldering eyes:

"Don't be afraid I'll stay. I'm going for a walk on the front of the island. That's as far away as I can get; I'd go farther if I could."

She passed out of the door and Stokes turned to the girl:

"There—that's what I was afraid of. Some of the rest of them may come in at any minute. We've got to get out of here, some place outside."

"The Point—the summer-house. I'll go down there now—you follow me."

She ran to the entrance, he at her heels. Walking leisurely up the path to the summer-house was Shine. She threw out her hands with a distracted gesture and struck a foot on the floor in a frantic stamp. Stokes smothered an oath. "Tell me here," she implored, but he answered with an imperative shake of the head.

"The garden." She was half-way across the room before he caught her up, and this time it was he who laid his hand on her arm:

"Sybil, have some sense. You'll get us in wrong every way. You don't want any of these people

to see us out there whispering together. That's
just the place they'll go while they're waiting
round for supper. Listen now, get a hold on yourself. Jim's safety is more important than your
anxiety. That photographer chap's just stroll-
ing round killing time; he'll move on from there
presently. Go up to your room and wait. You
can see the Point from your window. If he's gone
by seven, come down and go along to the summer-
house. I'll watch too and I'll meet you there."

She opened her lips for a last protest, then evidently seeing there was nothing else for it, gave
out a groaning "All right" and left the room. He
followed her, saw her mount the stairs, and walked
out on the balcony. It was exquisitely still, the
colors paling, the pines black and motionless as if
painted on the orange sky. He could see the figure of his wife moving slowly toward the ocean
bluffs. A newspaper lay on a table near him and
he took it up, slumping down in his chair as one
who relinquishes himself to a regained interest,
but he did not read.

VI

Anne packed for a space, then gave it up. She couldn't go on with it, she wanted to be downstairs, not lose one minute of the last evening at Gull Island. Her spirits, oppressed by Joe's behavior, began to bubble again, foam up in sparkling effervescence. You couldn't pack clothes in a trunk when you felt like dancing and the hour was too beautiful for belief and your lover might be waiting for you in the garden. She slipped off her negligée and chose her most becoming dress, leaf-green crêpe that made her look slim as a reed and turned her skin to ivory. She smoothed the black satin of her hair and hung round her neck the chain of green beads she had bought for a dollar but you'd never guess it. And she figured in front of the glass, studying her reflection this way and that, trying to see herself with new eyes

93

and judge if she was a girl a man might be proud
of.

While thus engaged she heard the chug-chug of
the launch. It must be Joe going, and anxious to
see the departure of that darkling and uncomfortable spirit she went to the window. It looked
out across the slant of roofs that covered the
kitchen wing and commanded a side-view of the
channel. Across the swift-sweeping current the
boat came into view, skimming forward like a
home-faring bird. Anne leaned over the sill, following it with startled eyes—where was Joe?
There was Gabriel in front at the wheel, but in the
back—she stretched her neck trying to see to the
bottom of the cock-pit, there certainly was no one
on the seat.

"Oh, *could* he have missed it?" she groaned and
cast up her eyes as if invoking the protection of
Heaven against such a calamity.

But he couldn't have, he wanted to go, it was
his holiday and he thought Gull Island was a
beastly hole. He must have been where she

couldn't see him. It was difficult to think where this might be—but he *might* have been bending down to put something in his suit-case. A chair could have hidden him. She remembered what he had said about leaving his baggage at the living-room entrance. If it was still there then he had missed the boat and she ran down-stairs, hoping with a prayerful earnestness that she would not find it. It was not there. "Then he *is* gone," she said to herself with a satisfied nod and drew a freer breath. The weight lifted, she went across to the garden where she might find Bassett, and as she covered the space between the doors the picture of the launch rose on her inner vision with Gabriel the only visible occupant.

Bassett was not in the garden, but Shine was, sauntering into view from the balcony end. He'd been loafing about he said, just come up from the Point. He'd been all round it, wonderful down there now and going to be more wonderful, and he pointed to a pale glow on the horizon where the moon was rising. They strolled about on the

lanes of turf between the massed colors of par-
terre and border, the air languishingly sweet with
the scent of the closing flowers. Then they went
in, luxuriously embedding themselves in two vast
armchairs. Bassett found them here and tried to
look genial at the sight of Shine. He'd been writing some letters in his own room and he dropped
into a third armchair with the sigh of well-earned
rest.

They talked about the moon and moonlight
effects. Shine wanted to take some photographs
after supper, get the pines against the sea and
the silvered bulk of the Point, and he spoke of his
flashlight picture which they'd have as a remem-
brance of Gull Island. Anne said that was a jolly
idea, but she didn't think they'd need a picture to
remind them of their stay, and she and Bassett
exchanged a smile.

It was still on their lips when a sound came
from outside, a single sharp detonation. It fell
upon the evening's tranquil hush, sudden and
startling, like something alien and unrelated.

"What was that?" said Anne.

"Sounds like a shot," Shine thought.

"It couldn't be!" Bassett got up. "Nobody has a pistol here and if he had he couldn't use it—one of the special stipulations Driscoll made when he lent us the place."

He moved to the land entrance and looked out.

"What could it have been?" Anne looked questioningly at Shine, who, having no other suggestion to offer, shrugged and shook his head.

The door of Mrs. Cornell's room opened on the gallery and Miss Pinkney emerged, Mrs. Cornell behind her.

"Mr. Bassett," she cried, a hand on the railing. "Where's Mr. Bassett?"

Bassett drew out from under the gallery and looked up at her:

"Did you hear that?"

"I did and I told you that Mr. Driscoll never allowed any shooting on the premises."

"Do you think that was a shot?"

"Well, what else was it?"

Mrs. Cornell, leaning comfortably on the railing, suggested that it might be an auto tire.

This drew a snort from Miss Pinkney:

"How'd a motor get here—swim or fly?" Then to Bassett: "Mr. Driscoll's very strict about that. He won't have the wild game or the gulls disturbed and——"

Bassett interrupted her:

"That's all right, Miss Pinkney. We were given those orders and we've obeyed them. And none of us could shoot here if he wanted to— there's not a pistol in the outfit. Don't you know it's against the law to carry one?"

"Then some one's taken mine," she exclaimed, and straightening up with an air of battle, "I'm coming down."

She left the gallery for the rear stairs, Mrs. Cornell in her wake.

"What does she mean—hers?" Anne asked.

"I don't know what she means," Bassett looked irritated. "It's the first I've heard of it."

"I don't see what there was to shoot at anyhow," came from Shine. "Looked to me when I was out there as if all the gulls had gone to bed."

Miss Pinkney, entering, focussed their attention.

"What's this about a pistol of yours?" Bassett asked.

She answered as she walked across the room to a desk under the gallery:

"It's the one Mr. Driscoll gave me, thinking it might be useful when I was here alone, opening or closing the house. I was to keep it loaded and have it handy, but I'd trust my tongue to get rid of any man and here it's lain with the poker chips." She pulled out a side-drawer of the desk. "There!" she exclaimed, turning on them in gloomy triumph, "What did I tell you! It's gone."

Bassett looked into the drawer:

"You're sure it was here?"

"Didn't I see it this morning when I put away the counters you were playing with last night?"

"Umph!" Bassett banged the drawer shut in

anger. "I'll see that this is explained to Mr.
Driscoll. And whoever's taken it, they'll get
what's coming to them. A damned fool performance! To get us in wrong just as we were
leaving——"

The hall door opened and Stokes entered.

"Who's shooting round here?" he said. "I
thought it was taboo."

"That's just what we want to know. Where
were you?"

"Sitting out on the balcony."

"See anybody?"

"No. I've been looking about. I went down
the path to the pine grove and round the house
but I didn't see a soul."

"Why, who could it be?" said Anne. "Aren't
we all"—she looked over the standing figures—
"No, we're not all here. Who's outside?"

"Mrs. Stokes is." Shine spoke up. "I saw her
walking along the ocean bluffs as I came up from
the Point."

"Sybil is, too," Mrs. Cornell added. "She went

out just a few minutes ago. I saw her from my window."

"It can't be either of them." Bassett's vexation had given place to a sudden uneasiness. "I don't understand. Nobody could have come over from the mainland with the tide up. I'll go out there——"

A sound from outside stopped him. It was a cry in a woman's voice, close by.

"What's that?" some one said, and before an answer could come, the cry rose again—a high wailing scream carrying words:

"Sybil! Sybil! Sybil's dead—Sybil's killed!"

A clamorous mingling of voices rose from the group, combined in a single up-swelling note of horror. The men rushed for the entrance and met Flora Stokes. She burst in between them, white as the ghost of Cæsar, with her opened mouth a dark cavity.

"Sybil's murdered—dead—shot." Each word was projected in a screaming gasp.

Bassett shouted at her, "Where?"

And she waved an arm toward the channel.

"There—from the Point. She's gone—she's dead! She went over into the water. On the top of the cliff. She's murdered—dead—murdered!"

As if she were dead, too, and of no more consequence, they fled past her—a line of people streaming out into the serene evening that held a hideous catastrophe. Only Anne stayed, her face as if overlaid by a coating of white paint. She went to Flora and seized her by the arm.

"Who was it?" she whispered. "Who did it?"

The woman looked at her at first as if not knowing who she was. Then jerking her arm free, clasped her hands against the sides of her head and went across the room staring upward and crying out:

"I don't know. I didn't see—— It's God's truth, I don't know."

Anne ran out after the others.

VII

THE moon had risen and hung on the edge of the sky like a great disk of white paper. Anne saw the others running this way and that along the edge of the Point. A boat was pushing out from the dock, Stokes in it, and, caught by the current, it shot down the gleaming surface of the channel. There were cries in men's voices and Stokes' answer, bell-clear from the water. Then Shine ran by her, back to the house, grim-visaged with staring eyes. The scene had the fantastic quality of a nightmare, the solemn splendors of the setting and the gesticulating, shouting figures darting about like grotesque silhouettes.

She ran on through the pine wood up the path beyond. Mrs. Cornell met her, tried to speak with chattering teeth, but ended in a scream and fell upon her shoulder. Over her head Anne saw Bassett flying down the slope to the wharf. Then presently boats moving out from Hayworth. They came with incredible speed, sliding forward in a group that spread and broke into units scattering across the channel. Here they sped back and forth, up and down, swift black shapes that seemed to be executing some complicated maneuvers along the glittering track of moonlight. She was aware of Bassett's figure leaving the wharf and racing to the house, of Shine thudding by and calling:

"They're here already! I got some one on the wire and I told him to go like hell."

Miss Pinkney's voice answered him from the edge of the Point where she stood like a black basalt statue:

"Oh, they're here, all right. Every feller that has a boat's out. But it's no use; no one who's ever got caught in *that* current's been found."

Shine muttered an invocation and came to a stop. They all stood speechless staring at the boats—the boats looking for Sybil who half an hour ago was alive like themselves and now was—where?

As soon as he saw the fleet in operation, Bassett ran to the house. He had to find Flora and get fuller information from her before he called up the police, and not seeing her outside, he supposed she was still there. The great room was almost dark. He felt for one of the standard lamps and pulled the string. The gush of light fell directly over her, close to him, sunk in an armchair, as still as if she, too, had ceased to live. He had expected difficulties in getting a coherent statement from her, but she told him what she had seen, briefly and clearly, as if she had known he was coming and was ready for him.

She had skirted the island and come to that part of the path which faced the Point. A hollow intervened, extending to the water's edge in a mass of shelving rock. Across this hollow she saw Sybil appear on the end of the Point, coming up from the opposite side, and almost immediately heard the shot. Sybil had thrown up her arms,

staggered forward and gone over the bluff. It all
happened in a flash and Flora, though describing
herself as dazed, had run down the path into the
hollow and out on the rocks thinking she could
catch her. But she saw the body go swirling by—
far out of her reach, caught and borne along in
the current. She had watched it, stunned, then
had come to her senses and staggered back to the
shore—she thought she had fallen more than
once—and ran to the house. On the way there
she had seen no one and heard nothing.

Bassett left her and went to the library to call
up Forestville, the county seat. He knew the
place well—a small town on the edge of northern
solitudes. It was the starting point for hunting
parties to New Brunswick, and Bassett, a sports-
man in his leisure hours, had stayed there several
times assembling his guides and gear. On his last
trip, two years ago, trouble with a guide had
brought him in contact with the sheriff, Abel
Williams. Over legal wrangling they had struck
up a friendship and he remembered Williams as

a man of some capacity, straight and fair-minded. If he was still in office it would simplify matters; to start out with confidence in the director would be a vital gain. He waited, the receiver against his ear, a foot drumming on the carpet, then a deep and growling voice hummed along the wire. It was Abel Williams.

Williams would be down as soon as he could, with Mr. Rawson, the district-attorney—an hour and a half to two hours, the roads being bad. The shore people had been told it was an accident—that's all right, couldn't hold an inquest anyway without a body and it was a good thing to keep 'em off. Better not let anything come out till they'd got the situation in hand, easy to fix at that end as the United American Press man was off fishing. They'd do a good deal better if the press was held off for a spell. The place was small, they'd clutter it up, tramp out foot-prints, get in the way searching for clues. Seeing where the island was and that there was no one on it but their own crowd, it would be possible to keep things out of the public eye till they had the work well started.

Bassett looked at his watch—nearly eight—probably two hours to wait. The best thing he could do was to get them together and keep them as quiet as he could. As he went down the path his mind collected and marshalled in order the facts he would have to present. They had all been in the house except Stokes on the balcony and Flora walking round the island. Stokes eaten into by a hopeless love, Flora on fire with jealousy and hate—passions that make for murder. "God, what's going to be the end of this?" he groaned to himself.

He found them in a group near the pine grove, excitedly conferring together. They had been back and forth to the house and the wharf, some aimlessly running about, others trying to do something intelligent and helpful. Stokes had just returned with the electric torch and they were preparing to search the ground for footprints. Bassett brought their activities to an end and shepherded them to the house. With dragging feet and lowered heads they trailed up the path and filed into the living-room.

Here, under the radiance of the lights, they looked at one another as if expecting to see startling changes and fell groaning into chairs, or sat, stiff and upright, with rigid muscles. The effect of the shock showed in Mrs. Cornell, Stokes and Shine, in a sudden outburst of loquacity. They went over and over it, what they were saying, where they were, what had entered their minds when they heard the shot. "And I thought to myself," sentence after sentence started that way. Then the feverish talk began to die. Bassett had told them when the authorities might be expected and as the hour drew near, dread of the drama in which they found themselves stilled their tongues. The sea breeze, freighted with the acrid odors of uncovered mud and seaweed, blew through the room. Bassett rose and closed the garden door, and eyes shifted to him, hung on his hand as it slid the bolt.

"What are you shutting the door for?" Mrs. Cornell quavered.

"I thought there was too much draught."

"Oh, what does that matter," she wailed, "with Sybil killed and floating out to sea?"

She broke into loud hiccoughing sobs. Stokes shifted in his chair and snarled out:

"Can't you stop making that noise?"

Bassett crossed to where Anne was sitting by the entrance. She had her back to the room and was looking out at the lights of Hayworth dotting the shore. He stood behind her chair and put his hand on her shoulder. Her fingers stole up and rested on his, icy cold. He bent till his head was close to hers and whispered:

"Bear up. Thank God this can't touch you in any way."

Her fingers pressed an answer but she said nothing.

Shine came toward them: "Those fellers were lucky who got off this afternoon. I might have gone with them if I'd had the sense."

Anne answered this time:

"Yes, they were more fortunate than we are."

Mrs. Cornell, her sobs under control, spoke up:

"But even if we *were* here they can't suspect us. We've got alibis, we're all accounted for. We were all in——"

She realized where she was going and stopped. There was a portentous silence. Shine almost shouted, pointing out at the channel:

"The tide's falling fast. They can't get into the dock here. How will they make a landing?"

Bassett answered:

"In a cove at the upper end of the island. They've a dock there for low water. They have to make a detour, that's all."

Flora, who had been sitting with her hand over her eyes, dropped it and sat erect. Her breath came from her in a loud exhalation that was almost a groan. Every pair of eyes shifted to her, watchful, questioning, apprehensive.

"Do you feel ill, Flora?" said Bassett, moving to her side.

"No—no," she looked wildly about. "But this waiting—it's so awful."

Miss Pinkney suggested a glass of water, but Flora waved a hand as if pushing it away. Stokes rose and moved to a seat beside her.

"They'll be here soon now."

She sank back and closed her eyes. Her husband bent a somber, sidewise look toward her, then laid his hand on one of hers. Her own turned and the thin fingers twined like clinging roots about his.

"It won't be hard," he reassured. "Just give them a clear account of what you saw."

She waved the other hand in front of her face, like a person in unendurable pain, who makes a vague distracted gesture for silence.

Anne spoke from the door:

"There's a light moving out from the shore."

The statement shook them. There was a simultaneous stir of feet and bodies, a heave of labored breaths.

Bassett went to the entrance:

"Yes—that's a launch. They're coming. I must go to meet them."

He looked over the company, the haggard faces all turned toward him. Some of them wore an expression of yearning appeal as if he was their only source of strength in this devastating hour:

"Now remember there's nothing to get scared or rattled about. They'll ask you questions and what you must do is to answer them accurately—not what you think or imagine but what you *know*. Keep that in the front of your minds. The clearer you are in your statements the quicker you'll get through. And please stay here, just as you are. They'll probably want to see you right off."

A benumbed silence followed his departure. Anne moved from the door to a chair nearer the others. Stokes withdrew his hand from Flora's and straightened himself, jerking down his waist-coat and craning his neck up from his collar. The low rippling murmurs of the receding tide were

singularly distinct. Suddenly the shrill whistle
of a launch pierced the night outside. Mrs. Cornell leaped as if the sound had been a weapon that
had stabbed her:

"Oh!" she cried, "why do they do that? Isn't
Sybil being murdered enough to stand!"

"For Christ's sake, keep your mouth shut,"
Stokes flung at her, glaring.

The savage quality in his voice penetrated Mrs.
Cornell's encasing terrors. She shrunk and slid
the look of a frightened animal at Shine. Then
the silence settled and they sat like those who have
looked upon the head of Medusa.

VIII

BASSETT on the wharf in the cove watched the launch approaching over the glistening floor of water. As it grated against the boards he heard his name in a deep-throated bass voice and the big body of the sheriff climbed over the side. A rough padded hand grasped his, and "Well, Mr. Bassett, the law's got us together again," was growled into his ear.

Two more figures followed him. One was Rawson, the district-attorney, whom the vivid light revealed as a man much younger than Williams, tall and narrow-shouldered, with a lean New England visage and a pair of horn spectacles astride a high-bridged nose. The other was disposed of with a casual hand-wave and a murmur of "Patrick," brought, it was explained, to take charge of the causeway. Rawson, it appeared, knew Gull

115

Island well, having been there several times on legal business for Mr. Driscoll.

As they walked back Bassett told his story. He noticed that the younger man's questions were sharp and to the point and before they had gone half-way realized that Rawson was of a much higher grade of education and intelligence than his coadjutor. A smart chap, he thought, and felt his burden lightened—they could do good teamwork. Stopping by the edge of the pine wood he pointed out the scene of the shooting and was again struck by the man's quick comprehension.

Moving on, Williams observed with grim relish:

"You couldn't have a murder committed in a better place than this—better for us. Once you're on here it's a damned hard business getting off. These folks are as good as in prison. Now, Mr. Bassett, just where does that causeway lie?"

The channel stretched before them, a shining expanse, ripple-creased, summits of rock emerging. The receding water was like a silver veil being slowly withdrawn, its delicate tissue torn by sharp-edged projections. Bassett pointed beyond the wharf:

"There! Below the water there are steps cut in the rock that lead down to it. It goes straight across to a breakwater and landing outside the village, a bank and a belt of trees above. The whole stretch won't be clear till nearly midnight."

Williams gave his instructions to the man Patrick—a watch on the causeway, any one stopped who came from the mainland or attempted to leave the island. Patrick, a silent massive countryman, with a stolid bull-dog face, thrust out his chin and nodded. He slouched off, the sound of his heavy boots loud on the rocks. The others turned toward the house, the light from its opened door falling outward in a long golden square.

The occupants of the room heard them and looked at one another. Mrs. Cornell, with clenched hands, slowly stood up, and the rest, like people in church who see a figure rise and simultaneously follow its example, got to their feet. They stood by their chairs, motionless, all facing the same way. It was like an ensemble scene in a theater.

The three men entered and under the shadow of the gallery paused for a moment surveying the standing figures much as they might have looked at some spectacle arranged for their approval. William was surprised at their number and their line ranged like a battle front. Rawson's sharp eye ran over the faces, mentally ticketing them, and Bassett, with no precedent to guide him, walked toward his associates and announced:

"Ladies and gentlemen, the authorities have come. Mr. Rawson and Mr. Williams."

They bowed and then not knowing what to do next, subsided into their seats. The men came forward, moving to the long table where Williams sat down, fumbling in his pocket for a fountain pen and paper and clearing a space for the taking of notes. Rawson, surveying the seated assemblage, said:

"This is the whole of your company, Mr. Bassett?"

"All who were here at the time of the murder. Several of the actors and assistants left at five-thirty and Joe Tracy, one of the company at a quarter to seven."

"You saw them go?"

"I saw the first lot go. I didn't see Tracy. But," he looked at Anne, "this is his sister, Miss Tracy. She probably did."

"Did you, Miss Tracy?" said Rawson.

Her voice was very low but steady and clear: "Yes, he went."

"Well, that disposes of them," said Rawson, and drawing up a chair, sat down facing the line of solemn people.

There were a few formalities to go through. A general agreement on the time of the murder—a few minutes before seven disposed of that, and the interrogation of Mrs. Stokes, the one eye-witness, followed.

She began well, telling the story she had told

Bassett. When she described her first view of
Sybil running to the edge of the Point, Rawson
interrupted with a question:

"Was she running fast, as if some one was
after her, as if she was frightened?"

"Yes, she was running fast but I don't know
whether she was frightened. I wasn't close
enough to see anything like that, and I didn't
have time to see. Just as I was looking at her
the shot came."

"Did you notice the direction it came from?"

"No—it was like a sort of loud snap in the air.
I heard it and she staggered along a few steps
and went, over."

"Did you hear any sounds—footsteps? A person makes a noise on this rocky ground."

"I didn't hear a thing." She leaned toward
Rawson with haggard insistence. "I *couldn't*
hear anything. I was stunned. Mr. Bassett
asked me that and you all seem to think I ought
to have heard the person—the murderer—or tried
to catch him. But I hadn't any sense, I just

stood there paralyzed, not grasping what had happened."

"Mr. Bassett says you went out on the rocks and tried to catch the body."

"Oh, yes. *Then* I came back to life. I ran down into the hollow and out on the rocks as far as I could go. And she was going by on the current—her hair and her dress all whirled about. Oh God, why was I the one to see it!"

Stokes addressed her, his voice low and urgent:

"Flora, just try to answer quietly."

She paid no attention to him, her eyes riveted on Rawson.

"And then you came back to the house?"

"Yes, but I stood there watching her for a few minutes. I don't know how long, desperate, not knowing what to do. And then I started to run back here and I fell down. I suppose I was shaking so and the rocks were slippery. I think I fell twice, but I don't know. I seemed to be half-crazy."

"You saw or heard nothing on your way back?"

"No, no, I keep telling you," her voice grew higher. "I *never* saw anybody. If anybody was there he must have been hiding. They could have heard me—I was screaming." She turned to the others. "Wasn't I screaming?"

Bassett confirmed her statement and she went on, her voice still higher, the cords in her neck starting out:

"Of course they heard me and hid—got out of the way. Some stranger. We were all in the house, everybody here was in the house. It couldn't have been any of them."

Stokes half rose: "Flora—*please!*"

She turned violently on him:

"Why shouldn't I say it? I'm not afraid. I was the only person outside and it couldn't have been me." She faced round on Rawson. "Nobody could think that. Ask them—these people. They'll tell you."

"That's not at all necessary, Mrs. Stokes." Rawson was mild and suave. "Now if you'll try to be calm——"

"Calm, calm," she groaned and bent almost double, dropping her face into her hands. Stokes got up, chalk-white in the lamplight:

"My wife's pretty well knocked out, Mr. Rawson."

"Quite understandable, Mr. Stokes. We won't trouble her any more just now. And if the rest of you ladies and gentlemen will refrain from saying what you think or offering suggestions we'll get on a good deal quicker."

Stokes took his chair. Flora raised herself and dropped against the back of hers with upraised chin and closed eyes. Bassett had a photographic impression of Williams, striking softly on his teeth with his fountain pen and looking at her.

They went on to Stokes who was very clear and composed. He had walked about—down the path to the pine wood and round that end of the house. It was absolutely still and he had heard nobody. He was not sure of the direction of the shot as he had been reading a paper at the time.

Like the rest of them he had had no suspicion of anything serious or, of course, he would have investigated.

Everybody else was in the house. Bassett indicated their positions, pointing them out as he explained their whereabouts.

Miss Saunders' movements followed. She had spent the earlier part of the evening sitting on the cliffs with Miss Tracy. Miss Tracy had left her some time after six, Miss Saunders saying she would follow but wanted to see the end of the sunset. No one had seen her come back but she had come back, for shortly before seven Mrs. Cornell had noticed her leaving the house.

Mrs. Cornell, invested with the grisly excitement of the hour, was eager to tell what she knew. She had been standing at the window of her room, and she saw Sybil on the path below passing the end of the balcony. Mrs. Cornell was surprised for it was not far from supper-time and Sybil was still in her Viola dress. She had not watched her, but had gone back to lock the trunk. Both she and Miss Pinkney agreed that the shot had followed soon after—about six or seven minutes they thought.

They diverged to the place of the murder, the Point. The last person who had been there was Shine, somewhere round six-thirty, though he couldn't swear to the time. He'd stayed there perhaps ten minutes, walking round, and had then gone up to the garden. As far as he could see the place was deserted. In answer to the question had he seen any one on his way back, he said he had seen Mrs. Stokes walking along the ocean bluffs and Mr. Stokes reading a paper on the balcony.

This ended the interrogations for the time being. The company was told they might retire to their rooms. But they were to understand that they were held on Gull Island for the present, no going off on any pretext or holding communication with any one on the mainland. Also—and Mr. Rawson was emphatic—once in their rooms they were to stay in them unless sent for by him.

He did not want any wandering about in the halls
or talking together.

They rose weariedly and prepared to go.
Stokes helped his wife to her feet and Bassett
edged between the chairs toward Anne.

"How are you?" he murmured, for her appearance shocked him.

"All right. There's nothing the matter with
me."

"Try to get some rest."

"Will they want us any more to-night?"

"I don't think so—not you anyway."

Stokes and Flora moved toward the hall door,
the woman limply hanging on her husband's arm.
Rawson's voice arrested them:

"Mr. and Mrs. Stokes, just wait a minute."

Everybody stopped in mid-transit, holding
their positions as if they were standing to be pho-
tographed.

"Where is your room or rooms?"

"We're together in a room on this floor out in
the hall here opposite the stairs."

"I'd rather Mrs. Stokes went up to the second floor." He turned to Bassett, "You have space up there I suppose?"

"Space!" It came from Miss Pinkney before Bassett had time to answer—these hirelings of the law did not realize where they were. "We've put up more people here than you could get into one of those flea-bitten hotels up your way."

"Take her things up there. You help her."

Flora turned stricken eyes on her husband. He said nothing but very gently loosened her fingers on his arm. They trailed away, Miss Pinkney stalking ahead. Mrs. Cornell and Anne made their exit by the opposite door. Both were silent as they climbed the stairs. Mrs. Cornell's door opened and closed on her, and Anne fared on to hers on the side stretch of the gallery. She looked down into the lighted room, saw Shine move toward the entrance, heard his voice, loud and startled:

"Why, there's some one down by the dock!"

The other men wheeled sharply, on the alert. She stopped, head bent, listening.

"Patrick—the damned fool." It was Williams. "Told to watch the causeway and standing up there like a lighthouse."

"Oh, it's your man. I'll go down and tell him." Shine wanted to help all he could before his retirement to the butler's bedroom. "He ought to be where he won't show, is that it?"

"Yes, tell him to stow his carcass somewhere out of sight. He ain't there to advertise the fact he's on guard."

"If he gets in the shadow under the roof of the boat-house," said Bassett, "he can command the whole length of it and not be seen from either side."

"That's the dope. The neck of this bottle's the causeway and it's going to be corked good and tight to-night."

Anne's door closed without a sound.

The three men turned back from the entrance. "Is that woman gone up-stairs yet?" Rawson murmured to his assistant as Williams stepped to the middle of the room and watched the gallery.

He continued to watch it till Flora and Miss Pinkney appeared and finally were shut away behind their several doors, then he looked at Rawson and nodded.

"Now," said the district-attorney to Bassett, "I want you to show me where that pistol was."

Bassett indicated the desk:

"In the third drawer of the desk. Miss Pinkney is certain it was there this morning."

"And you know it wasn't there when you looked after the shooting?" Rawson went to the desk as he spoke.

"I can swear it wasn't."

Rawson pulled out the drawer and thrust in his hand.

"Well, it's here now," he said, and drew out a revolver.

He held it toward them on his palm. They stared at it, for the moment too surprised for comment. Rawson broke it open; there was one empty chamber.

"Can we get into some room where there's more

privacy than this place?" he said. "I want some more talk with you, Mr. Bassett."

Bassett directed them to the library. He put out the living-room lights and followed them.

IX

Bassett was prepared for what he had to tell.
During the long wait for the officers of the law
his mind had been ranging over it, shaking bare
from unnecessary detail the chain of events that
had ended in murder. It was impossible to con-
ceal the situation between Sybil and the Stokeses;
he could not if he had wished it and he did not wish
it. A girl had been brutally done to death, a girl
innocent of any evil intention, and his desire to
bring her murderer to justice was as strong as
either Williams' or Rawson's. And they could get
the facts better from him than from the muddled
stories of the others, their minds clouded by prejudice and hearsay. He hoped that what he said
would be coldly unbiased, the naked truth as he
knew it. That his revelations would involve a
woman whom he liked and pitied would not induce

131

him to withhold what ought to be known. Chivalry had no place in this grim drama. As he had discharged his duties as director of a theatrical company rent by passions and dissensions, he now prepared to discharge them as the most responsible and fair-minded member of the group.

Sitting by the desk in the library he unveiled the situation, what he had heard, seen and knew. The men gave an unwinking attention, now and then stopping him to plant a question. The trend of Williams' thoughts was soon revealed— he suspected Flora Stokes. When the matter was threshed out he came to an open admission with the remark:

"Well, you have only one person here who had the provocation necessary to commit murder."

Bassett made no answer. If his duty required him to tell all he knew, it did not require him to give his own opinions.

Rawson who was smoking, his long, loose-jointed frame slouched down in an armchair, took his cigar from his mouth:

"Of course the woman's the first person you'd think of. She had the necessary provocation and the state of mind. But the way she came in and told them—as Mr. Bassett describes it—doesn't look to me like a guilty person."

"Why not?"

"Sounds too genuine, too like real excitement."

"Don't you think it's natural to get excited if you've killed some one?"

"Yes, but not just that way."

Williams leaned over the arm of his chair:

"You got to remember something about these people, Rawson—and it counts big—they're all actors."

Bassett spoke up quickly:

"No, she wasn't acting. You'd have known that if you'd seen her. What she did was natural—a woman suffering from a fearful shock."

"Couldn't an actor put that on?"

"Yes, some could, but I'm certain she wasn't."

"When Stokes came into the room after the shot," said Rawson, "how did he behave?"

"He seemed all right. But I can't honestly say that I noticed him much. The light was fading and I was so irritated by the thought that some one had been shooting that I didn't pay any attention to him."

"Oh, rubbish!" Williams made a rolling motion in the scoop of the big chair. "You can't suspect the man; he was in love with her. He didn't want to kill her, he wanted to keep her alive."

"Men *do* kill the women they love, especially when they can't get her."

"Yes, they do. I've known of such cases. But that's impulse. This was premeditated." The sheriff pointed at the revolver lying on the desk. "Sometime to-day somebody located that gun, took it for a purpose—not to shoot sea-gulls as you thought, Mr. Bassett."

Rawson looked at the pistol:

"Premeditation, all right. Was there anybody in the outfit who didn't know you'd opened that drawer and found the revolver gone?"

Bassett considered:

"Stokes didn't know. He came in after I'd shut the drawer. I didn't speak of it because just as I'd got through asking him if he'd seen any one, we heard Mrs. Stokes' scream."

"And *she* didn't, of course," commented Williams.

"While you were running round at the Point the house was empty?"

"I think Mrs. Stokes was here all the time. I never saw her outside."

"Any of the others come up?"

"I'm not certain of all of them. I know Shine did; I sent him back to phone over to Hayworth for the boats. And Stokes did, he came up for the electric torch when I was in here telephoning to you."

"Then neither of them knew the loss of the revolver had been discovered and they had plenty of opportunity to return it to the desk?"

Bassett nodded, and after a minute's cogitation Rawson went on:

"Doesn't it seem odd to you that no one saw Miss Saunders when she came back to the house?"

"No. They were all in their rooms, except Shine who was down at the Point and Mrs. Stokes who was reading on the balcony. I asked her particularly if she'd noticed Sybil pass and she said no, she'd been interested in her book and wouldn't have noticed anybody."

"I'd give a good deal to know what Miss Saunders did in that time. I think it would let in some light."

"How so?"

Rawson narrowed his eyes in contemplation of an unfolding line of thought:

"Well, what took her out again to the Point after she'd come in? She hadn't a good deal of time and she wanted to change her clothes before supper. It looks to me as if she met some one in the house, some one who wanted her to go down there with them."

"Mrs. Cornell says she was alone."

"She might have started alone and gone to meet them."

"Then it couldn't have been Stokes," said Williams, "for Mr. Bassett says she wouldn't speak to him if she could help it."

"That's right," Bassett nodded in agreement. "She'd never have made a date with him. She shunned him like the plague. If you knew her you wouldn't see anything in that going out. She was restless and unhappy and the place here—the sea, the views—fascinated her. It was our last evening and it was like her not to want to miss any of it, slip out for a minute to enjoy the end of it."

"And came upon some one waiting for her—lying in wait and——"

Rawson did not finish. A thud and crackling crash came from the living-room. The three men rose with a simultaneous leap and ran for the door.

X

Of all the people gathered in the house that evening Anne had been the most silent. Her ravaged face, the contours broken by gray hollows, bearing the stamp of shock and horror, had been unnoticed among the other faces. Now and then a pitying glance had been directed to her, grief as Sybil's friend must have added a last unbearable poignancy to the tragedy.

After her question to Flora her mind had seemed to blur and cease to function. She had run from the house not knowing what she did, gone hither and thither with the others, looking, speaking, listening in a blind daze. It was not till they returned to the living-room that her faculties began to clear and coordinate. The lights, the familiar setting, the talk that could not leave the subject, shook her back to reality. It was

138

then that she went to the window and sat with her back to the room. She wanted no one to see her face; she was afraid of what it might betray.

Her thoughts circled round the image of Joe as she had last seen him—the vision of him as some one strange and sinister. And the boat— the boat with only Gabriel in it—it kept coming up like a picture revolving on a wheel—going and returning, going and returning. Had he stayed and what for? That question revolved with the picture of the boat. She could not get free of them, their obsessing force held her like a somnambulist staring into the night.

She thought of telling Bassett and gave that up—with the police expected she could not get him alone, and why add to his burden with her suspicions? Yes, that was what it was—nothing but a suspicion. She had no certainty, Joe might have been in the boat, Joe might have got off the island some other way. To-morrow something might come to light that would make these hideous fancies seem like the dreams of delirium.

That was the state of mind she tried to maintain
when she went up-stairs and overheard a man was
on guard at the causeway.

With that knowledge her outlook changed. Her
passive rôle was over. She sat down on the side
of the bed and with a grim desperate resolution
faced what she had tried to flee.

If Joe had done it and if he was on the island
he would try to get off at low tide. It was safe
to assume that he was outside, hidden till the
causeway was open. To go out to find him would
be useless, he would never reveal himself to her,
and if. she was seen suspicion would instantly be
aroused. She must get somewhere that would
command the causeway and its approaches. Her
mind ran over every nook and angle, every shadow
and rock ledge between the house and the shore.
Impossible—it was too open and the light was
like day. The best place—the only place—was
the living-room entrance. From there she could
see in all directions, the balcony end, the kitchen
wing, the pine grove. She would try to wave him

back, possibly get to him—she had to take her chances and trust to Heaven.

And then he might never come—it might be just an awful nightmare and he was with Jimmy Travers on his way to the northern woods. She dropped her face in her hands and sent up broken words of pleading that it might be so.

The tide was at full ebb at midnight. At a quarter before she made ready. She took from the bureau a book she had been reading—if she met any one she could say she had come down to find it—and opened her door with the stealth of a burglar. A dead silence reigned as she stole down the stairs and into the living-room. Here the great line of windows—the moon not yet upon them—shone in gray oblongs diffusing a spectral light that did not touch the darkness under the galleries.

At the entrance, pressed against the door, she looked out. It was a world of white enchantment, breathlessly still. She could see the patterned surfaces of leaves, the cracks and fissures of the rocks. Below the channel lay almost bare, pools glistening like dropped mirrors, mounds of mud casting inky shadows. In the middle—a restless silvery sparkle—ran a narrow stream carrying a glinting line of radiance to the ocean beyond. The pungent smell of mud and seaweed came from it along with the sleepy lisp of rippling water.

She could hear the murmur of the men's voices from the open library windows, and like the throbbing of a muffled engine, the beating of her own heart.

Into that deep enveloping quietude came a sound, so faint, so infinitely small and hushed, that only expectant ears could have caught it. It came from the room behind her, and turning, she slid back against the wall, her body black against its blackness. The sound continued, the opening of a door opposite, the door into the kitchen wing. It seemed no door in the world had ever opened so` slowly—creaking, stopping, resuming, dying away. She could see nothing, for the darkness of the gallery lay impenetrable over that furtive entrance.

There was a footstep, light as the fall of a leaf, and she saw him coming toward her in that high luminous pallor from the windows. He was like a shadow, so evenly dark, a shape without detail, moving with a shadow's noiseless passage. She saw the outline of the cap on his head and that he carried his shoes in one hand.

She came forward with a hand raised for caution, sending her voice before her in an agonized whisper:

"Go back, Joe. The causeway's watched. You can't get over that way. *Go!*"

He was gone, a fleet flying, vanishing back into the darkness under the gallery. Out of it came the soft closing of the door.

The room swayed, pale light and darkness swam and coalesced. She knew she was near a table and put out her hand to steady herself by it, something solid to hold to for one minute. The polished surface slid under her fingers and she groped out with the hand that held the book. The book slipped from her clasp, fell with a thud like a thunderclap, and a grasping snatch to save it swept a lamp crashing to the floor. Panic dispelled her faintness and she made a rush for the door. She had gained it. Her fingers clutched round the knob, as she heard the steps of the men in the hall and knew it was too late to escape.

They burst in, thrust into the room's dim quiet as if shot by a blast.

"It's nothing," she called, hearing her voice thin and hoarse. "Nothing's happened. It's only Anne Tracy."

The lights leaped out and she saw them, Bassett with his hand on the electric button, stricken still, looking this way and that. His eye found her first, backed against the door, a small green-clad figure with an ashen face.

"What's this mean?" said Rawson.

"Nothing." She was afraid the handle would rattle with the shaking of her hand so let it go. "I upset the lamp in the dark. I didn't see it that's all."

"What are you doing here?"

"I came down to get my book. I forgot and left it when I went up-stairs."

She could get her breath now and her voice was under control. She felt strength oozing back into her body and with it courage.

"You're as white as a sheet," Williams blurted out.

"Did something frighten you?" demanded Bassett.

"No, but a sort of faintness came over me, there by the table, and I grabbed at it and upset the lamp."

Rawson looked at the table with the shattered fragments of the lamp beside it. It was not far from the entrance door.

"Did you see anything—anything outside?"

"No, not a thing and I didn't hear a sound."

"What do you suppose made you feel faint?"

"Oh!" She dared to make a gesture, upraised hands that dropped limply. "Hasn't there been enough here to make anybody faint?"

"You've got to remember, Rawson," said Bassett who thought the man's insistence unnecessary, "what a shock this has been—especially to Miss Tracy who was Miss Saunders' friend."

"I remember." Then to Anne: "Miss Tracy, if you should withhold any information from us you'd get yourself into a very uncomfortable position."

"I wouldn't, I wouldn't," she breathed.

Rawson's glance remained on her, dubiously intent. Bassett noted it with a resentment he found it difficult to hide.

"You can absolutely rely on Miss Tracy," he said. "She would be perfectly frank with you if she had anything to tell."

"No doubt, no doubt," said the other, and walked to the entrance. "I'm going out to have a look around." On the sill he turned and addressed Anne. "I gave some instructions to you ladies and I expected to have them followed. You'll please remember them in the future."

He passed out into the brilliancy of the moonlight. Now that he was gone Bassett felt he must

make her understand. He had been astonished at
what she had done. It was so unlike her, a dis-
obedience of orders at such a time as this.

"You must do what they tell you, Anne. They
have to make these rules and it's up to us to keep
them."

"I will now. You can trust me. Mr. Williams,
you can see how it was. I couldn't sleep and my
mind was full of this awful thing, and I thought if
I could put it on something else—get free from my
thoughts even for a few minutes!"

Williams grunted his comprehension. He felt
rather tenderly toward her, she looked so small
and wan and her voice was so pleading.

"Where was your book?" he asked.

"On the table behind you. I was feeling round
for it and I think I pushed it off with the lamp."

"What was the name of it?"

"*Victory*, by Joseph Conrad."

He went to the table. His back turned, she
and Bassett exchanged a long look. Williams
picked up the book and came back with it.

"Here it is," he said, giving it to her. "And just make a note of the fact that you're not to go round the house at night after books or anything else."

She assured him she would not, she would give them no more trouble, and opening the door she slipped away. They remained without speaking till she came out on the gallery and walked to her room. Bassett stood looking up after she had disappeared, the memory of her face as they burst in upon her added a new peculiar distress to his harrowed state.

"Well," said Williams, "her book *was* there."

Bassett stared at him:

"*Was* there! Why shouldn't it be?"

Williams gave an upward hitch of his shoulders:

"Words come easy, Mr. Bassett."

"Good God!" exclaimed Bassett in horrified amaze. "You have any idea she was *lying?* If you have, get it out of your head. I've known Miss Tracy for three years and she could no more say what wasn't true than—well, she *couldn't,* that's all."

"I don't think she did. It sounded to me a perfectly straight story."

"It was. You can take my word for that."

They were back in the library when Rawson reappeared with Shine. Shine, unable to sleep, had been sitting by his window when Rawson, scouting, had stopped to inquire if he had seen any one. Shine had not, but had volunteered to join in a hunt and the two had been about the house and the immediate vicinity. Nothing had been discovered and Patrick had seen no sign of life or heard no sound. Now they had come back for the electric torch and were going to extend their search. A person concealed on the seaward side of the island might be moving at this hour when the causeway was free. Bassett said he would go with them and the three men left the room by one of the long windows.

Williams opened the library door and turned off the lights. The noise of the departing trio would suggest to any one on the watch that the house was free of police supervision and there might be developments. He took the desk chair as easier to rise from than the deep-seated leather ones and settled himself to a *resumé* of what they had so far gathered.

He was convinced of Mrs. Stokes' guilt and ran over the reasons. A hysterical woman, frantic with jealousy—that alone was enough. But that woman had been the only member of the party who at the time of the shooting had been some distance from the house. She had taken the pistol with the intention of using it if an occasion offered. Her walk had been undertaken with the hope that she might find that occasion in the hour before supper when they were all in their rooms. The occasion *had* offered. Miss Saunders, unable to resist the beauty of the evening, had gone to the Point alone. He set no store by Rawson's opinion that the woman's state of mind was too genuinely distracted. He considered it as part of a premeditated plan carried through with nerve and skill.

She would have known that the report of the pistol would have been heard at the house. This,
when Miss Saunders did not return, would have
suggested foul play. And she, Mrs. Stokes, was
the only person out on the island. A later entrance, with an assumption of ignorance, would
have turned suspicion on her like a pointing
finger. She was too intelligent for that—had
called her abilities as an actress to her aid and put
them all off with her screaming excitement.

Another point that he wanted to look into was
the length of time she had been at the shore after
the report—a great deal too long for what she
said she had done. Too paralyzed to think or
move, her explanation was stunned. Williams
was divided in his opinion as to that—either pulling herself together for the grand-stand play she
was to make or possibly pushing the body into
the water.

It was at this juncture that he suddenly cocked
his head and let his hands drop softly to the arms
of the chair. From the stairs outside came a

faint creak, a pause and then again, step by step a bare or stockinged foot in gradual descent.

The big man arose as noiselessly as he could and made for the hall. But his bulk and his boots were not adapted to rapid movements or silent surprise. As he reached the hall he heard the pattering flight of light feet and cursed under his breath as he felt for the electric button. Her room—the one he had seen Miss Pinkney put her in—was just beyond the stair-head to the right. And her husband's—he turned and faced the secretive panels of its closed door.

Williams dropped his head and trod thoughtfully back to the library, but this time he left the hall lights on. Also he lit the library ones and allowed himself the solace of a cigar. "She won't try that again to-night," he said to himself and dropped into an easy chair.

Then Stokes must know. They had had opportunity for private conference in that hour after the murder when the others were out of the house. She had either told him or he had accused her; for

all they knew he might have seen her do it. Anyway she wanted to get speech with him and it
might be support, counsel, the matching up of
their stories—but whatever it was she must have
been in dire straights to take such a risk.

Williams smoked on, comfortably sprawled in
the deep chair, thinking out a line of attack on
the Stokeses.

XI

THE night search of the island had given up
nothing and a daylight exploration was set for
the morning. Before this, however, Rawson
wanted to go through Miss Saunders' room, which
by his orders had been locked and left untouched.
It occupied the corner of the second floor directly
above the library, the first of the long line of bed-
chambers that stretched across the land front of
the house. Their doors opened upon a hall that
traversed the building from end to end, its central
section forming one side of the gallery.

In her short stay the girl seemed to have impressed the place with her dainty charm. It was
beauty's bower, a bright and scented nest, chintz
hung, with white fur rugs on the floor and silken
cushions which bore the impress of her light
weight. Steeped in the morning sun, warm and

still, it extended its welcome as if waiting for her entrance. The signs of feminine occupation caught the eyes of the men and held them chilled on the threshold. Enhancements of her beauty were strewn on the bureau, the garments that had clothed her graceful body lay on the bed where her hand had thrown them. A delicate perfume filled the air, the fragrance of her passing habitation still lingering in ghostlike sweetness after the living presence had gone.

Rawson moved first, shaking off the spell. He looked into the open wardrobe trunk, completely packed but for the last hanger. "Going to put her costume there," he said, touching it with his index finger. He pulled out the drawers and ran his eye over their contents. A gray crêpe dress lay across the foot of the bed, beside it a cloak and a black hat with a water-lily garnishing the brim. "These," he said, "were the clothes left out to wear."

Bassett nodded. He could see Sybil in the gray dress with her hair a golden fluff below the edge of the black hat. She had worn them on the way up and been pleased when he had admired her costume.

They went over the desk; a few postage stamps and a writing tablet. But the desk had evidently not been used—the square of new blotting paper in the carved leather holder was unmarked. The waste-paper basket only contained a torn veil and the wrapper of a package of hair pins. On the bed-table was a book and a candy box containing two chocolate bonbons.

By the bureau an open bag stood on a chair. There was nothing in this but a book, one of the many treatises on self-development and the achievement of spiritual calm and control. Poor Sybil! Bassett turned away with a sick heart— had she found now what she had been striving for?

The dressing-table was the only place in the room that her neat arranging hand had not touched. It was covered with a litter of toilet articles, cold-cream jars, rouge boxes, powders and scents, a silver hand mirror, a pair of long white gloves. Williams picked up a bead bag and opened it. It contanied a wisp of handker-chief, a bunch of keys, a lip-stick and a gold change purse. In the central compartment were three five-dollar bills and in the gold purse one dollar and thirty-five cents in coin.

"This couldn't have been all the money she had," he queried.

"Why not?" said Bassett. "I guess some of us haven't that much. She didn't need any. All our expenses were paid and she was going straight home. One of those bills was probably intended for Miss Pinkney."

Nothing more came to light. The closets were empty, the bathroom contained a few toilet ar-ticles and a nightgown and negligée hanging on the door. Obviously a place swept clean for a coming departure by one who had no premonition that that departure would be final.

They passed out and along the hall, Rawson wanting to see the disposition of the passages and stairs. At the door next to Miss Saunders' he stopped, asking who occupied that room. It was vacant now but had been Joe Tracy's. He opened the door and looked in upon another chintz-hung chamber, all signs of recent habitation removed that morning by Miss Pinkney's energetic hand. A steamer trunk in the corner caught his attention and Bassett explained it was young Tracy's trunk which his sister was to take back to New York with her.

Beyond that the hall ran into the gallery passing under an arch of carved wood. They traversed it, looking down into the richly colored expanse of the room below, and fared on under a companion arch into the last stretch of the hall. At the stair-head Rawson halted:

"Only two flights connecting with this floor, the one in the front by the library and this. Now the top story—how do you get to that?"

Bassett showed them a staircase at the end of the hall. He had never been up there himself, but some one, Mrs. Cornell, he thought, had. It was the servants' quarters and had not been occupied during their stay, Miss Pinkney and her helper having had rooms on the gallery.

Later on they would take a look up there, the island was their business now. According to Williams, all this searching was merely a formality, and they descended the stairs conferring together. It was their purpose to keep Stokes and his wife from any possibility of private communication. Shine had been delegated to stay beside one or other of them, and so far, they had made no attempts to get together. Their amenability added to Williams' suspicion and it was his suggestion that they should bring Stokes with them on their hunt. When that was finished they planned taking Mrs. Stokes to the place of the murder and making her rehearse just what she had seen.

Starting from the Point they explored the island foot by foot, scouting across the open expanses where a rabbit could hardly have hidden and prying into the hollows and rifts of the boulders on the shore. On the sea front, wedged

between miniature cliffs, there were triangles and
crescents of sand, bathing beaches with small pa-
vilions built against the cliffs. But no footprints
marred the sand's wave-beaten smoothness, no
trail of broken grass and brambles indicated the
passage of a body. The path that followed the
bluff's edge, making a detour round the ravines,
yielded neither trace nor clue. The dressing-
rooms back of the amphitheater behind a clump
of cedars, gave no sign of having harbored an
alien presence. The little amphitheater itself,
sunk in its green cup, lay open to their eyes as
they stood on its brink. They walked among the
stone seats, seamed with a velvet padding of moss,
and gathered up a few programs, a pair of woman's gloves and a necklace of blue beads.

That brought them to the end. The house had
no outbuildings; garages, barns and sheds were in
the village across the channel. There was no one
in hiding on the island.

They found Flora, Shine and Mrs. Cornell on
the balcony. As they came up Flora looked at

them and then averted her glance as if in proud
determination to show no curiosity. Rouge had
been applied to her cheeks and her dry lips were a
vivid rose color. The high tints showed ghastly
on her withered skin but her dark eyes were scin-
tillant with an avid burning vitality. It was like
a face still holding the colors and hot warmth of
youth suddenly stricken by untimely age.

Williams, halting at the foot of the steps, told
her what they wanted—her position and Miss
Saunders' at the time of the shooting, going over
the ground and making it clear to them. She rose
alertly with a quick understanding nod—she
would be glad to, it was her earnest desire to be
of help to them in any way she could. Rawson
noticed that she did not look at her husband but
kept her eyes on Williams with an intent frowning concentration, moving her head in agreement
with his instructions.

At the shore she was eager to explain everything, took her place on the path where she had
been when she saw Sybil appear on the other side

of the hollow. Her rendering of the scene was graphic and given with much careful detail. The men, grouped about, followed her indicating hand, stopping her now and then with a question. Stokes stood back watching, his face in the searching daylight smoothly yellow like a face of wax.

Williams' questions were many and pointed, and it soon became evident to Bassett what he had in his mind—that her explanation of her actions did not account for the length of time she had been on the shore. Whether she saw it or not he could not tell; checked in her story she would answer patiently, reiterating her first statement that her stunned condition had robbed her of the power of thought or motion. But he was sure Stokes had grasped the trend of the query; he drew nearer, his flexible lips working, the hand hanging at his side clenching and unclenching. Once he assayed to speak, a hoarse sound throttled in escape. It pierced the strained attention she was giving her questioners, and, for the first time, she hesitated and fumbled for her words.

When it was over and they returned to the house, Stokes dropped to her side and drew her hand through his arm. She drooped against him; her narrow body looked nerveless, as if but for his support it would have crumpled and sunk. But he planted his feet with a hard defiance, each step drew a ringing echo from the rocks and he held his head high. Bassett, following them, noted his rigid carriage, and when he turned his profile, the wide nostril spread like that of a winded horse.

There was a ghastly lunch. The men of the law ate greedily and without words. Shine was ashamed that he had any appetite and tried to appease it with bread which he could extract from the plate in front of him without notice. There was almost no speech. Miss Pinkney, executing her duties with an automatic precision, did what waiting was necessary, and her voice, inquiring their needs and proffering second helpings, broke desolate expanses of silence.

When it was over Williams and Rawson took up the trail again. They were now going to direct their attention to the Point, especially the summer-house, from which a path led to the summit of the bluff whence Sybil had fallen. Bassett, who had hoped to get a word with Anne, was bidden to join them, and the three left the house step by step tracing the passage of the dead girl.

They began with the pine grove. Needles carpeted the ground, slippery smooth, a beaten trail winding between the tree trunks. Beyond it the path ascended the bare slope to the summer-house. "No place to hide here," Rawson said. "The murderer, if Mrs. Stokes' story is true, was either in the open or in the summer-house." They paused, moved on, bent for a closer scrutiny of the dry grass, searched for an imprint in the pebbled walk. Secretive as the rest of the island, the way divulged nothing. Sybil's light foot had made no faintest mark, she had gone to her death leaving no track nor trace.

The summer-house, a small, six-sided building, was covered by a thick growth of Virginia creeper that swathed its rustic shape. In four of its walls the vines, matted into a mantle of green, had been cut away to form windows. Framed in these squares sea and land views were like pictures brilliantly bright from the shaded interior. The other two sides held the entrances, one giving on the path that descended to the pine grove, one to its continuation to the Point. A circular seat ran round the walls and a table in the same bark-covered wood was the only movable piece of furniture. This was drawn up against the seat at one side. Rawson moved it out as the other two ran exploring eyes over the walls, the door-sills and the floor of wooden planking upon which a few leaves were scattered.

"Here," he cried suddenly. "What's this?" and drew from a crevice where the legs crossed, some scraps of a coarse gold material.

He held them up against the light of the opening—three short strands of what might have been the gilt string used to tie Christmas packages.

"What do you know about this?" he said, offering them to Bassett's gaze.

Bassett looked, and Williams with craned neck and lifted brows looked too. They were exactly of a length, broken filaments of thread attached to the end of each.

"They've been torn off something," Rawson indicated the threads, "caught in that joint of the table legs and pulled off. Did she have anything like this on her dress anywhere, a trimming or——"

"Fringe," Bassett interrupted, "the fringe on her sash."

"Ah!" Rawson could not hide his exultation. "*Now* we've got something we can get our teeth into."

"Yes." Bassett took the pieces and studied them in the light. "That's what it is. She wore a wide sash round her waist with ends that hung down edged with gold fringe. This is a bit of it."

"Well," said Williams, "that's a starter anyhow. She was in here."

Rawson sat on the bench and drew the table into its former position:

"It not only proves she was in here, but it proves a good deal more. This is the way she was, with the table as we found it close in front of her. The ends of her sash would have been in contact with the table legs. Now she jumped up quickly—do you get that? If she'd gone slow or had time to think she'd have felt the pull and unloosed the sash—but she sprang up, didn't notice." He looked from one to the other, his lean face alight.

"Frightened," said Bassett.

"So frightened she didn't feel it, and moved with such force she tore the fringe off. That scare took her up from the seat and sent her flying through the doorway for the Point."

"Hold on now," said Williams. "If she was as scared as that why didn't she go for the house where there were people?"

"Because she was too scared to think. Some one with a pistol was on the other side of the table." He rose and went to the entrance facing the Point. "And the person with the pistol shot at her from here—winged her as she ran." He turned to Bassett. "That's why you saw no one when you looked out after you first heard the shot. The murderer was in here lying low."

"Yes." Bassett thought back over the moment when he had stood in the living-room doorway. "That's the only place he could have been or I'd have seen him. But they wouldn't have been any time together—couldn't have had a quarrel or a scene. According to Mrs. Cornell it was only six or seven minutes after she saw Sybil go out that she heard the shot. That would give them only two or three minutes in here."

"Time enough to draw a gun and back it up with a few sentences. It bears out what I've thought from the start—not an accidental meeting but a date, to which the woman came unsuspecting and the other primed to kill."

"Then Mrs. Stokes got on to that date," said Williams, "and broke in on it. And there's only one person that date could have been with—Stokes."

Bassett's nerves were raw with strain and anxiety. This reiteration of a rendezvous with Stokes maddened him:

"But it couldn't have been. I've told you. I knew Miss Saunders well. I know what she felt about the man, and besides I have the evidence of my own eyes that she avoided him in every way she could. Make an appointment to meet him alone! She'd as soon make an appointment with Satan."

Neither of the men answered him for a moment. Williams regarded his sentiment with respect. He had been a friend of the dead girl's and it was natural he should stand up for her, whether rightly or wrongly Williams was not yet sure. Rawson was impressed; he had formed a high opinion of the director's candor and truthfulness and his words weighed with him:

"I go a' good deal by what you say, Mr. Bassett, and as to this meeting of which I'm convinced—whom it was with I don't know. Williams here has made up his mind and worked out

his case. I don't agree with him. I believe Mrs.
Stokes is telling the truth. What she says hangs
together all right. I think her explanation of the
passage of time when she was on the shore is entirely plausible. That she may know something is
possible, but I don't think she's guilty."

"Then you must think it's Stokes," said Williams with some heat. "There's nobody else it
could be."

Rawson considered before he spoke:

"I don't see Stokes as deliberately murdering
the woman he was in love with. That's generally
an act of, impulse, sudden desperation. And
there was no impulse here. Careful premeditation—the stealing of the revolver, luring her to
this summer-house, the threats or rage when she
got here that made her fly. It's more like the
working out of revenge than the act of blind passion. Stokes doesn't look to me the kind of man
that would kill so carefully. He's too soft."

"Then who is it?" Williams exclaimed. "Somebody killed her."

Rawson moved toward the doorway:

"That's about all I'm willing to agree to at present. But I'd like to see Stokes again. He and his wife may know more than they say—I don't deny *that*—but she's got a better nerve than he has. We'll get him into the library and have a whack at him."

XII

BASSETT was detailed to find Stokes and bring
him to the library. A summons from the director
would have an air of informality which might put
Stokes off his guard. Rawson did not communicate this to his messenger, but told Williams
when they were alone. He had been watching
Stokes and thought the man showed signs of
strain. That morning at the beach Stokes' manner and appearance had suggested a nerve tension
which might rise from anxiety about his wife, but
might also be the result of some knowledge he was
struggling to withhold.

Bassett found Flora and Shine on the balcony
and heard that Stokes had gone to his room to
try to get some sleep. He knocked on the door
and to a gruff "Come in" entered to find Stokes
lying on the bed. He rose quickly, exhibiting the

same alacrity his wife had shown earlier in the
day.

"Of course," he said. "I'm ready to come
whenever they want me. In fact I've been lying
here expecting it, going back over last evening,
trying to think of anything I may have overlooked
that might help them."

There was a willing bruskness in his manner,
an almost hearty readiness to do what was asked
of him that seemed not quite genuine, adopted,
perhaps, to hide the natural nervousness of a person in his position. Seated in an easy chair before the two men, Bassett back of them by the
window noticed that his hands were restless,
smoothing and pulling at his clothes, settling his
tie. Despite his disquiet he assumed an attitude
of expectant attention, gravely awaiting their
will, his eyes glancing from one face to the other.
He might readily have been a guilty man primed
for attack, or an innocent one shaken by the un-
toward circumstances in which he found himself.

Rawson's manner was friendly and reassuring.

They wanted to get all possible information on the movements of the company the evening before. Last night the examinations had been cursory and fuller ones were necessary. They would like to know just what he had done from the time he entered the house to change his clothes to the time when he had heard the shot.

He answered promptly with businesslike directness. Went to his room, changed his clothes, laid on the bed resting for a while, then sat on the balcony reading the paper.

While he was sitting there Miss Saunders must have passed the end of the balcony by the path that led to the Point.

She must have, but he had not seen her, being occupied with his paper.

Had he while in the house seen Miss Saunders or heard her voice?

He had not. He had no idea she had come in.

Had he seen his wife?

"My wife? Yes, I saw her for a moment. In the hall when I came out of our room after dressing."

"Did she tell you she was going to take a walk round the island?"

"Well, I hardly remember." He tilted his head sidewise with an air of careful consideration. "Yes, I believe she did say something about it— it's very vague in my mind. It made no impression on me. We exchanged a few words and parted."

"She said nothing to you about Miss Saunders being in the house?"

"Why no, she didn't know it. We didn't mention Miss Saunders at all."

"But she was—she had been—a frequent subject of conversation between you?"

His eyes, looking at Rawson, seemed to harden and grow more fixed:

"We *had* talked of her—naturally being in the same company."

"Your wife and Miss Saunders were not very friendly?"

A fierce light rose in the fixed eyes, the nostrils widened.

"What are you getting at, Mr. Rawson?"

"Our business, Mr. Stokes. We're here to investigate a murder and we can't spare people's feelings or shut our eyes to disagreeable facts."

"Have I shown any signs of expecting that? I've put myself at your disposal, my wife has. We're ready to give you any help we can, but I'm not ready to back up any damned suspicions that have been put into your mind."

"We're not asking you to," said Rawson. "But we know what was going on here before the shooting."

Bassett spoke up:

"I'm the person that told them, Aleck. It had to be done. They had to be acquainted with the whole situation, and they got it from me. But they heard no lies, no suppositions—you know you can trust me for that."

Stokes' glance shifted to him. Through its savage defiance Bassett could detect the torment of his soul, despairingly betrayed to the one person he knew would be just.

"Oh, I'm not blaming you," he answered: "You couldn't do anything else. And they can hear it all from me." He looked at the two men. "I don't want to keep anything back. You don't have to use any of your third-degree methods with me. I'm willing to tell. I was in love with her, madly, like a fool, hounded her, dogged her footsteps. You've heard that. And my wife was jealous—so jealous they all could see. You've heard that too."

The confession of his passion, remorseless in its bitter revelation, was horrible, like the tearing aside of wrappings from a raw wound.

"Yes, we've heard it," muttered Williams.

"She hated me. I don't know whether you've heard that too, but I'm telling you and perhaps you'll believe what I say if it's against myself. She hated me, and I wouldn't let her alone. My wife was jealous. Do you see—is it clear? Oh, we're in damned bad, my wife and I, but we're not in so bad as you're trying to make out." He jumped to his feet, the shine of sweat on his forehead.

"I don't see, Mr. Stokes," said Rawson quietly, "where you get that. We haven't made out anything yet."

"Oh, I can see. We were the only people outside the house—that's enough to build a theory on. And motives—who had a motive? That's the way you go to work. Find a motive, fit some one to it. My wife had a motive, that's sufficient. Don't ask what kind of woman she is, don't look any further, you have to get some one and she's the easiest. Christ!" he cried, throwing out his arms with a dramatic gesture, "it would make the gods laugh!"

"Mr. Stokes, if you'd take this calmly——"

"Calmly! Seeing what you think and where you're trying to land us! But just let me ask you something." He thrust his head forward, the chin advanced, the eyebrows in arched semicircles rising almost to his hair. "Do you happen to remember there were five hundred people on the island that afternoon? Any kind of person could have been here on any kind of errand."

Rawson answered with a slight show of impatience:

"Just leave our business to us, Mr. Stokes. You're here to answer questions."

"Oh, that's plain—questions all pointing one way. But there were other people on the island besides that crowd—besides us—who might have had a motive. Isn't anger a motive?"

He projected the sentence with a malevolent force, the words enunciated with an actor's incisive diction.

"Anger!" ejaculated Williams. "Where does that come in?"

"Here, on Gull Island. Oh, we've had more than jealousy. Rage and spite will go as far. Take your eyes off my wife and me for a moment—look somewhere else."

Rawson's face showed no surprise, blankly inscrutable, but Williams wheeled in his chair and turned an expression of startled inquiry on Bassett. Bassett, in his turn, was staring in astonishment at Stokes.

"What are you talking about?" he said. "Rage and spite—whom do you mean?"

"I mean Joe Tracy," was the answer.

"Joe Tracy!" exclaimed Williams, looking vaguely about in a baffled searching of memory. "Who's he?"

"Good God, Aleck!" Bassett made a step forward: "Get a hold on yourself—think of what you're saying. He wasn't here, he'd left the island before that."

Stokes paid no attention but went on, glaring into Rawson's expressionless face:

"A damned devil of a boy with a record. Ask him," he pointed to Bassett, "ask any of them what kind he was and how he acted here. It isn't I alone that saw it. Yesterday morning at the rehearsal he'd have struck her if Bassett hadn't interfered. What was the matter—I don't know. I don't pretend to know everything, but I know rage and hate when I see them."

"Aleck, you're crazy," Bassett's voice was raised in exasperated insistence: "He'd *gone*."

"Couldn't he come back? Aren't there boats to be hired at Hayworth?" He turned to Rawson. "I don't accuse him, I'm not like you, I don't jump at conclusions, point and say 'There's the murderer!' But I want a square deal and I won't get it till you've looked up Joe Tracy. Call your dogs back from the scent they're on and put them on his. Justice—that's all I ask for—justice for my wife. For myself——" He stopped. His excitement seemed suddenly to die. He looked old and wearied, his body relaxed, the fire in his sunken eyes extinguished in a profound gloom. "It doesn't matter what happens to me. I've thrown everything away—and Sybil's dead."

There was a slight pause. Rawson broke it, clearing his throat and rising from his chair:

"That's enough for the time being, Mr. Stokes. You can go now, if we want you we'll call on you later!"

Without a word Stokes turned and left the room. When the door had closed on him Bassett said:

"He's out of his mind—Joe Tracy—when he knows he wasn't here."

Williams gave a bearish shrug:

"Oh, pshaw, what's the matter with him's easy to size up. Breaking down, losing his nerve. Whether he knows his wife did it or not he sees everything points there and he's just laying hold of anything to mark time. They go like that— I've seen 'em before."

Rawson, who had been standing with his hands deep in his pockets and his eyes fixed on the floor, moved to the chair:

"Let's hear about this boy, Mr. Bassett—all this anger and hate business he's been buzzing round."

He sat down and lit a cigar. Through the smoke he watched Bassett with a narrowed glance as the director unfolded the story of Joe, the quarrel and Sybil's accusation.

When it was over Rawson knocked the ash from his cigar, meditatively looking at the crumbling gray heap:

"Are you under the impression, Mr. Bassett, that her story was true—that the boy *had* been spying on her?"

"I don't know. Of course she was in a high-keyed emotional state that might engender unjust suspicions. On the other hand you couldn't trust his word, and there was big money offered."

"And when you returned to New York you would have found it out."

"Yes, I told him that."

"And he would have realized that it would go hard with him, where you were concerned, and with the rest of the profession?"

"Yes, he'd know. She was very popular and there was a general sympathy for her. Any one acting against her interests would have met with a pretty cold reception."

Williams stretched and rose from his chair:

"Well, it's all right to gather up everything, but it doesn't get us any further. If the boy'd been here, seeing what he was and how he felt, there might be something in it. But as he got out before the shooting it leaves us just where we were before. What do you think about going up and looking over that top story—routine business we ought to get through."

"Not now," Rawson moved to the door. "I'm going across to the mainland."

"Mainland—what's that for?"

"Look up some things—that boy's movements for one. I'll take Patrick and the launch and send him right back. The causeway's covered so we don't need him there. If Mr. Driscoll ever wanted to sell this place I'd recommend it for a penitentiary, save the state some money, only want guards twice in twenty-four hours. Come down to the dock with me, Mr. Bassett, and tell me which way Tracy was going."

Bassett went with him feeling for the first time that he could give information with the tranquillizing assurance it would react on nobody. When he left Rawson at the dock he went to look for Anne.

XIII

To THE outside eye Anne had presented no
more dolorous and dejected an aspect than any of
the others. If she could not eat, neither could
they, and if she sat sunk in somber gloom they
either did the same or gave expression to their
nerve-wracked state by breathless outbursts of
speech. No one, not even Bassett, noticed that
Anne's demeanor was in any way other than what
might have been expected.

Had they been able to see into her mind the
group at Gull Island would have received its second staggering shock.

She kept as much to herself as she could without rousing curiosity. She had to think and to
be alone where she would focus her thoughts, hold
them trained on what she knew and what might
develop. She wanted to keep her mind on the
main issue, inhibit any fruitless speculations,

185

wait and be ready. Joe was on the island and with the guarded causeway would stay on the island till after they had gone. Her hope, giving her strength to go through the automatic actions of behavior, was, that suspicion not being directed to him, he could lie hidden till they left and then make his get-a-way. She knew that Gabriel had gone to White Beach for a week's deep-sea fishing, and Gabriel was the one person besides herself who knew that Joe had not crossed to the mainland. They surely would be moved away before a week and if, during that time, the belief that he had gone remained unshaken, he was safe.

So far she was confident that no suspicion had touched him. She did not see how it could. They were all satisfied that he had left, her answer to Rawson had been accepted in good faith. There would be no investigating of his movements for there would be no reason for doing it. He had passed outside the circle of the tragedy, was eliminated as the actors were who had gone on the earlier boat.

If they didn't find him!

Where was he? He had entered the living-room by the door that led to the kitchen wing and rear staircase. That would look as if he was in the house. But she knew that no doors were locked on Gull Island and that he might have come from outside, choosing a passage through the darkened building rather than expose himself to the moonlight. If he was in the house he must be in the vacant top story and she was certain—every sound of heavy footsteps had been noted by her listening ears—that the men had not been there yet. That would argue that they felt no need of hurry. Were they taking things in a leisurely way because of their assurance that no one could escape, or were they so convinced they had their quarry that no further search was necessary? What conclusions were they coming to behind the closed doors of the library—had they fixed on some one of the party, the obvious ones, Flora, or Stokes?

She checked these disintegrating surmises, drew

her mind back with a fierce tug of will. That
would come later. If Joe got away she would tell,
confess it all, go to jail. It didn't matter, what
happened then. Only what was here before her
counted now.

When the search of the island started she went
up to the side of the gallery that skirted the line
of windows. From there she could command the
whole seaward sweep of its ten acres. She would
be alone here, secure against intrusion; she could
drop her mask, let her face show what it might,
not watch from beneath her eyelids for the questioning looks she dreaded.

The group of men came into her line of vision,
moving across the flat land between the house and
the ocean. She sat crouched, watching with set
jaw. Presently they dropped over the edges of
the cliffs, then inarticulate surges of prayer rose
in her, blind pleadings; and, her hands clasped
against her breast, she rocked back and forth as
if in unassuagable pain. But they always reappeared without him, went down again, came up,

scrambling through the stony mouths of ravines—always without him. When they returned
to the house, she fell back in the chair, her eyes
closed, whispering broken words of thanksgiving.

With her breath and her voice under control
she went down-stairs. She knew now that he must
be in the house.

After lunch she drifted out on the balcony with
the others and from there saw Bassett and the
two officers of the law go down the path to the
pine grove. Following Sybil's movements on the
Point—that would take them some time. Mrs.
Cornell said she was going to the kitchen to help
Miss Pinkney (if it wasn't for that work she
thought she'd go crazy), and she advised Anne to
go up-stairs and lie down.

"You look like the wrath of God, honey," she
said, hooking her hand through Anne's arm and
drawing her with her. "You can't sleep, no one
expects that of you. But stretch out on the bed
and relax—you get some sort of rest that way."

Anne went with her, Mrs. Cornell's step drop-

ping to a crawling pace as they crossed the living-
room, her arm drawing Anne closer, her hearty
voice dwindled to a whisper:

"Do you know anything?"

"No, how should I?"

"I listen all I can but they're as tight as clams
when we're around. I think they've got a hungry
sort of look as if they were on some trail. Haven't
you noticed it?"

Anne hadn't noticed anything.

"Well, I have. I sit there slumped together and
acting helpless, but I'm not like the Foolish Vir-
gins—my lamps are lit."

"Do you think they have any one in mind?"

"They have two, dearie, as we all have." They
had reached the door and she opened it warily.
"And one moment I'm thinking it's one and the
next moment I'm thinking it's the other and the
third moment I'm thinking it's neither of them."

They passed through the doorway and went
down the hall, stopping at the foot of the stairs.
Mrs. Cornell offered a last consoling word:

"You can be thankful for one thing, Anne, Joe's not being here."

"Joe?"

"Oh, I'm not saying he had anything to do with it. But these cases—you read about them in the papers. Every little thing traced up. And she and Joe having been at loggerheads they'd be pouncing on that—not telling you anything, sending up your blood pressure with their questions. You're spared that and it's worth keeping your mind on. Nothing so bad but what it might be worse."

She went on down the hall. Anne, on the stairs, waited till she heard the sound of the opening door and Miss Pinkney's welcoming voice, then she stole upward very softly. She did not go to her room as Mrs. Cornell had advised, but tiptoed to the end of the hall where the staircase led to the top story.

She ascended with delicate carefulness letting her weight come gradually on each step. Despite her precautions the boards creaked. The sounds seemed portentously loud in the deep quiet and she stopped for the silence to absorb them, and then, with chary foot, went on. At the top she stood, subduing her deep-drawn breaths, looking, listening.

The middle of the floor was occupied by a spacious central hall furnished as a parlor and lit by a skylight. Giving on it were numerous small bedrooms, the doors open. They were like rows of neat little cells, all the same, bed, dresser, rocking-chair, with a white curtained window in the outer wall. The windows were open, the sashes raised half-way, and the fresh sweet air passing through fanned the muslin curtains back and forth in curved transparencies. Anne remembered Miss Pinkney saying something about opening the top-floor windows to air the servants' quarters before the house was closed for the season.

The stirrings of the curtains, billowing out and drooping, were the only movements in the place. She moved to the middle of the room and sent her voice out in a whisper:

"Joe, Joe—are you here? It's Anne."

Her ears were strained for an answering whisper, her eyes swept about for a shape creeping into view, but the silence was unbroken, the emptiness undisturbed. She entered the rooms, peered about, opened cupboards, looked for signs of occupation. Again nothing—vacancy, dust in a film on the bureau tops, beds untouched in meticulous smoothness.

One door was closed, near the stair-head. Opening this she looked into a store-room, a large, dark interior lit by two small windows. They were dust grimed, and the light came in dimly, showing upturned trunks and boxes, pieces of furniture, lines of clothes hanging on the walls.

"Here," she thought, and with her heart leaping in her throat, crossed the threshold:

"Joe, it's Anne. I've come to help you."

Nothing stirred in the encumbered space, no stealthy body detached itself from the shadows.

"Oh, answer me if you're there!" Her voice rose the shade of a tone. It came back from the raftered roof in smothered supplication; the silence it had severed closed again, deep and secretive.

She feared to stay longer and slipped, wraith-like, down the stairs. In her room she sat down and considered. He must have been there. Where else could he be unless in one of the unoccupied apartments in the lower floors. But he hardly would have dared that with people coming and going. He had been afraid, doubted her as he had always done, or possibly found a hiding-place too shut away for her whisper to penetrate. To-night she would have to get food to him, take it up when the men were in the library and the others safe in their rooms.

She could do nothing more and went down-stairs in the hope of seeing Bassett. Since morn-ing she had longed for a word with him. Through the darkling obsession of her fears he loomed as the one loved and familiar being in a world where she fared in solitary dread. Not that she had any idea of telling him, the direful secret was hers alone to be confessed later on some awful day of reckoning and retribution. But she wanted to see him, get courage from his presence, feel the solace of his arm about her. She was so lonely with her intolerable burden.

The living-room was empty, but listening at the hall door she heard the murmur of men's voices in the library. They were in conference again and might be long. She passed out into the garden and sank down on one of the benches. The air had grown chilly and a little wandering breeze was abroad. It moved among the flowers and sent shivers down the great wisteria vine trained up the house wall and ascending to the chimneys. She looked at it, its drooping foliage, stirred by a quivering unrest, showing the fibrous branches intertwined like ropes—an old vine such as city dwellers seldom see. She tried to fix her attention on it, picturing it when the blossoms hung in lilac cascades, a riot of color from ground to roof. But her mind was like the needle in the compass, inevitably swinging back to the same point.

There were clouds in the sky, hurrying white masses driving inland and carrying the breath of fog. They had blotted out the sun and were sweeping their torn edges over the blue. If they kept on it would be dark to-night—no moon—but there was the man at the causeway.

She sat with drooped head immersed in thought, her hands thrust into the pockets of her sweater. It was thus that Bassett found her. Life leaped into her face at his voice and she stretched a hand toward him.

"Oh, I've been hoping to see you," she breathed, already trained to a low wariness of tone.

The words, the gesture, pierced his heart. She looked so disconsolate, so wan, her face the pallor of ivory, her black hair always shining smooth, pushed back from her brow in roughened strands. He had charged himself to keep from her any knowledge of the interest in Joe, but had he been of the loose-tongued sort that unburdened itself, the sight of her devastated beauty would have sealed his lips.

He sat down beside her and took her hand in his. In her turn she had been shocked by his appearance, worn, his ruddy firm-fleshed face riven with lines.

"I thought I was never going to get a word with you," he said. "This is the first moment I've had. How are you?"

She asserted her well-being, and he studied her face with anxious eyes.

"Dear Anne," he murmured, and lifting her hand, pressed it to his lips. The two hands remained together, the woman's upcurled inside the man's enveloping grasp.

"That faint feeling last night, I suppose that will bleach you out for a while?"

"Oh, I'm all over that. It was a crazy thing for me to do, going down and then knocking the lamp over. They didn't think anything of it, did they?"

"Anything of it? Why no, what would they think? You explained it to them and they were satisfied with what you said. And afterward I told Williams that he could absolutely trust your word."

"I gave a great deal of trouble and——" Her voice was husky and she cleared her throat. He was worried by the coldness of her hand and sought to warm it by enclosing it more tightly in his. After a moment she went on:

"I suppose you can't tell me anything—anything of what they're doing?"

"No. It's all a mess so far—feeling about in the dark—nothing sure."

"But they must be feeling about after some one?"

"Darling, what's the good of talking about it? It's only going round and round the same subject like a squirrel in a cage. We don't get many minutes together and we don't want to spoil them. Let's try to forget just while we're here."

"Forget!" she exclaimed. "Nothing would make me do that but being dead myself."

She leaned her head on his shoulder and drew her hand from his to clasp it round his arm. He said nothing for a moment, perturbed by her words and tone. He had thought of getting her away, having her moved to Hayworth. Now he felt he must do it at once, the shadow of the tragedy was too dark on her spirit.

"I've got to get her out of here if I go to jail for it," he said to himself. "She can't stand much more of this."

She too was silent for a space, stilled by the attack of a sudden temptation. His tenderness had weakened her, the gulf between them seemed too much to bear when the way was so perilous to travel alone. She wanted to be close to him again, break down the barriers and extend her arms to him for succor and support. He would calm the upwellings of terror that rose in her, perhaps have some man's solution for her desperate problem. The desire to tell him gripped her, undermined her will like a disintegrating drug. She did not dare to broach it suddenly, sense enough remained in her to go carefully, step by step.

"I wonder if any one here *does* know something and is keeping it back."

"It may be—too frightened to speak."

"Well, if they did—I mean something that looks suspicious, might be a help—they'd be expected to tell, wouldn't they?"

"If it were anything definite. Just to take up their time with a lot of vague surmises is the last thing they want. People get stampeded in a case like this, butt in with all sorts of silly leads and theories." He gave her an uneasy side glance. "Are you imagining that you know something you ought to tell?"

"No, oh, no. But I keep thinking of it, all kinds of possibilities."

"Can't you stop thinking of it? I wish you would."

"Oh, Hugh, how can any one? It fills up your mind so that nothing else can get in. It would be so terrible to have to confess something against another person."

He nodded and murmured, "Terrible, all right."

"I don't see how one could do it. Now, you, if you were in that position—had suspicions of some one?"

"I don't tell them, that's not my province. I'm here to assist, not to direct them."

"Just say what you're sure of?"

"Exactly. What I know, what I can vouch for as fact. I wish to God I *could* furnish some that would lead us in the right direction."

She said nothing, her cheek against his shoulder, her head bent down till her face was hidden from him. He looked at the grass at his feet in hárassed survey of his obligation:

"I'm the only person here they know anything about, that they care to trust. It's a devilish position, trying to hide what you think, trying to state only what you know, fairly, without personal feeling or prejudice. But it's up to me to do it till we round up something. I don't want to get anybody in wrong, but, good lord, if I knew any one was—didn't guess, was *sure* of it—I'd give the information up just as quick as I could get across to that library."

Her hope was over and she saw now how wild it had been. With a heart like stone she sat by him, feeling the contact of his body, his arm pressed against her side, knowing herself as far removed from his comfort and help as though an ocean lay between them.

The light in the garden was fading, an even soft dusk was gathering. There were no splendors of sunset to-night, day was dying without ceremonial rites. The hurrying clouds had thickened and were a sagging gray pall with rays of fog drifting below. Suddenly the doorway of the living-room sprang into the dimness, an illumined square, and Miss Pinkney was visible moving about lighting the lamps.

"No moon to-night," said Bassett, and getting up, drew her to her feet. "Come, let's go in. It's too chilly for you out here."

It was not till they had gathered round the supper table that Rawson's absence was revealed. Miss Pinkney, coming in with the teapot, saw the empty chair and frowned. Though subdued, her spirit was not broken, and she could not tamely submit to these minions of the law disregarding the meal hours.

"Is Mr. Rawson coming to his supper?" she remarked with an acid note.

"Mr. Rawson's away on business," Williams answered. "You can keep something for him."

No more was said and the meal proceeded on its dismal way.

XIV

AFTER supper Bassett and Williams retired to
the library. They were surprised and intrigued
by the length of Rawson's absence. He had been
gone over two hours and what could have held him
on the mainland so long was difficult to imagine
unless a new lead had developed. This was Bassett's idea, also his hope. To have suspicion
lifted from Flora would be the first lightening of
the grinding distress he had felt since the murder.
Williams wondered if he could have come on anything about Joe Tracy; but Bassett shook the
suggestion off with a shrug. He could check up
on Joe in half an hour; besides, there was nothing
to be looked for in that line. His confidence was
not assumed, his mind was untroubled by any
fears about Joe. That something had turned up
which might head the chase in a new direction was

so encouraging a thought, that, by contrast to his sensations for the last twenty-four hours, he felt almost cheerful.

In the relaxation of the strain he was conscious of fatigue for the first time. He threw himself on the sofa and in a moment had sunk into the deep deathlike sleep of exhaustion. Williams, sitting near the telephone also nodded, his big body sagged together in the chair, his chin embedded in his chest.

The group in the living-room, viewed by the uninformed spectator, might have been the usual evening gathering of an informal Gull Island house-party. They had shut the garden door against draughts and with the inland entrance open wide the place was scented with a sharp sea tang and cool with the breath of the ocean. The tide, full-brimming, lay a dark circle about them, no moonlit path or silvered eddies to-night, the channel a solid swath of black between them and the clustering shore lights.

They made a deceptively quiet picture, pleas-

ant, agreeable-looking people resting in reposeful
attitudes after a day in the open air. Shine was
looking at a book of engravings spread on the end
of the table. Mrs. Cornell had brought in Miss
Pinkney after the business of washing up—Mrs.
Cornell found Miss Pinkney's society so fortifying
that she sought it at all hours—and together they
made a feint of playing a double solitaire. Anne
and Flora sat near by reclining in armchairs, both
silent, with the fixed eyes of preoccupation.
Stokes was the sole member of the company whose
inner unrest broke out in movement. He paced
back and forth before the fireplace, quick long
strides over the bear rug to the hall door and back
again. Once or twice the edge of the rug caught
his toe and he kicked it out of his way with a
violent angry jerk of his foot.

When the minutes ticked away and no one came
to overlook or overhear, a cautious trickle of talk
began to flow. Question and answer crossed, low-
toned, interrupted by warning looks at the hall
door. Where had Rawson gone, what could he be

after? That the question lay uppermost in all
their minds was shown by the quick response to
the first, murmured tentative, the comprehension
of sentences left unfinished with only the query in
the eyes to point their meaning. The drooping
attitudes gave place to a tense eagerness of pose,
heads thrust forward on craned necks. Shine forgot his book, the cards lay scattered beneath the
hands of Mrs. Cornell and Miss Pinkney, and
Flora edged her chair closer. Their voices,
hushed by fears, were fused in a murmurous hum,
rising as the subject swept their interest higher,
checked in sudden minutes of listening alarm.

Rawson must have got hold of some information, gone afield on a new clue. Then followed
speculations, surmises, suggestions—wild, fantastic, probable. It might have been nothing Shine
thought, simply a trip to the county-seat on business connected with the case. At this Anne crept
into the circle of lamplight, nodding an avid
agreement. Stokes coming forward caught his
foot in the edge of the bear rug, stumbled and

broke into a stream of curses. Miss Pinkney, who thought oaths anywhere reprehensible and on Gull Island profanation, grimly bade him lift his feet. He glared at her, more curses imminent, and Flora groaned, clutching the arms of her chair and rolling her eyes upward.

"For God's sake don't mind anything anybody says," implored Mrs. Cornell slapping her hands down among the cards. "This is a murder case, not a social function."

They calmed down and presently, with no more ideas to exchange, grew silent listening for the returning launch. It was a listening so wrapt that the room became as still as a picture and they as motionless as pictured figures. The ticking of the clock was audible, the sucking clinking sounds of the water along the shore. The significance of what they awaited grew with the minutes till the coming of the launch seemed an event of fearful import upon which their fates hung.

The entrance of Williams shook them from their terrors. If his face told them nothing, his manner was kindly gruff—they must be tired, best thing for them to go to bed. As they rose and trailed limply to the doors he beckoned Shine to remain. He would want him later, had a job for him, so he'd better go now and get some sleep. His room was on that floor, the butler's? All right, he'd find him. Shine departed, grateful. He was half-dead with sleep, but had kept it hidden as he had his hunger, regarding both as unmanly weaknesses in the hour of calamity.

Williams went back to the library where Bassett still slept. He looked at his watch—a quarter to nine. He couldn't understand it—what could Rawson have got hold of on the mainland when it was as plain as printing Mrs. Stokes was the guilty party. He started and moved to the window; the throbbing beat of an engine came through the silence, a low spark of light was advancing from the opposite shore.

When he heard the boat grinding against the wharf he waked Bassett.

"Rawson's coming. And it's nearly nine."

Rawson came in by the window, his eyes blinking in the room's brightness. He came briskly, with something of theatrical effect in his silent entrance, his purposeful walk to the desk. Bassett at once noticed a change in him, a suggestion of enhanced forces, of faculties recharged with energy. He tried to look stern but satisfaction shone in his eyes and lit his long lantern-jawed face. He was like the bearer of good tidings who would have worn the high smile of triumph if a smile were fitting.

"Well," said Williams, "where the devil have you been?"

"Down the coast, twenty-five miles, on roads that would have put anything but a flivver out of commission."

"You got something?"

"I did—this time. We're on the right track now if I'm not much mistaken."

Williams gave an incredulous grunt. He did not believe in new material and in advance placed himself in stubborn opposition:

"What did you go down the coast for?"

"To find a man called Gabriel Harvey."

Bassett, about to sit down, stopped in surprise:

"Gabriel Harvey?— That's our launchman."

"Exactly. And I had a devil of a time to find him. Down in a place called White Beach, hidden away with friends in a shack without a telephone."

"But why——"

"I'll tell you." Rawson dropped into the desk chair, and, his elbows on the arms, leaned forward, his eyes behind their glasses traveling from one face to the other. "I went over there to look into Joe Tracy's movements. I couldn't find any one who'd seen him come ashore and learned that the man Gabriel who took him over, had gone to this place White Beach for deep-sea fishing. Not being able to get hold of him I went to the station to see if I could gather up anything. And I did. The baggage man told me Gabriel had been there before he left for White Beach leaving a suit-case and fishing-rod to be held till Tracy called for them. They're there now. I saw them."

Williams said nothing, not ready with argument till more was divulged. Bassett, in blank amazement, ejaculated:

"Why, that's the most extraordinary thing——"

"Wait, Mr. Bassett," Rawson raised a long commanding hand. "I hung round till the evening train came in; that's the train Tracy was to take. I saw the conductor—it's a small branch road and travel is light at that hour—and he remembered his passengers, two women and a child. Those were the only people who left Hayworth on the seven-fifteen, the last evening train. I went back to the village and made inquiries. Tracy had hired no vehicle at the garage or livery stable, nor had he been seen anywhere about the place. Then I got a car and went to White Beach. I was some time locating the old chap, but I finally ran him down. He said he had not taken Tracy across to the mainland last night."

Rawson dropped back in his chair. In answer to Bassett's expression he nodded soberly:

"Yes, it's a pretty queer business. Gabriel said he'd told the boy to be on time; made it clear to him that he wouldn't wait. When Tracy was not on the wharf he went to the house to look for him, saw his bag and fishing-rod in the doorway and took them. No one was about and he left— not sorry, I inferred from what he said, to give 'the young cub' as he called him, a lesson."

Bassett got up:

"But it's incomprehensible," he exclaimed. "I can't make head nor tail of it. No one ever questioned that he'd gone."

"No one said they'd seen him go but his sister," came from Williams.

Bassett wheeled on him:

"Yes, you asked her. Didn't she say she'd seen him?"

"No." Rawson's voice was dryly quiet. "I've thought of that. What she said was that he went. In all fairness to her she probably thought so— took it for granted as you all did—that he'd gone."

"But why? What's the meaning of it? If he'd missed the boat he'd have turned up, he'd be here now."

"Oh, he didn't miss the boat," said Rawson.

"Well, then, what was he doing? What made him stay?" In the turmoil of his amazement, this sudden precipitation of a new mystery, Bassett had not yet grasped the sinister trend of the other's thoughts.

"Why," said Rawson slowly, "he might have been staying for a purpose."

"What purpose?"

"Can't you imagine a purpose, Mr. Bassett?"

"Good God, you don't mean to say you think he *did it?*"

"I'm not saying anything yet. But I'd like you to tell me how you explain it. He says he's going, leads every one to think he's going, makes all the preparations for his departure, then secretly, without divulging any change of plans, doesn't go. Aren't those actions—well to put it mildly—questionable?"

"Yes—the whole thing's inexplicable as we see it now."

"And note this. He had cause for anger against Miss Saunders—she'd given him away to you—and you yourself have told us that he had an ungovernable temper."

"He had a devilish temper and a damned mean disposition and I make no doubt he was blazing mad with her. But that he'd go to work to kill her in cold blood, lay in wait for her—no—you can't make me think that."

"Same here," said Williams. "You ain't got enough provocation. With Mrs. Stokes you have—a woman jealous of her husband."

"And you've got a man," retorted Rawson, "moved by one of the passions that lead oftenest to murder—revenge."

"Revenge?" echoed Williams.

"Miss Saunders' accusation, if true,—and I think it was,—would ruin him in his profession. He learned what she'd done to him just before he was due to leave."

A chill passed through Bassett—revenge was a word that fitted Joe. But he cast the thought out, moving away from the desk and exclaiming with angry repudiation:

"Oh, it's unthinkable, preposterous."

"What but an evil intention could have made him act as he did?"

"Any number of things. It may be a prank—a practical joke we'll get an explanation of later. He may have invented the story of his fishing trip and gone off with a girl."

"Had he a girl?"

"I don't know—also he may have done something dishonest, got in wrong some way—he was capable of it, I'm not defending him—and been frightened and lit out."

"How did he get off?"

Bassett's voice was raised in his exasperation:

"Good lord, Rawson, we weren't jailed here then. He could have had a boat hidden in one of the coves. This place wasn't escape-proof till you turned up. He could have rowed ashore and landed anywhere, and that's what he's done."

"Unless he's here."

"Here on the island?"

"That's my opinion, in hiding on the island."

Williams spoke with an air of patient reminder:

"Ain't we gone over it with a fine-tooth comb?"

Rawson pointed to the ceiling:

"How about that top story? A person—we won't say who—could have killed the woman, entered the house while the rest of you were on the beach, put back the pistol, and gone up-stairs."

Williams made a motion to heave himself up from his chair.

"Well, if that's how you feel about it let's go up and have a look for the person."

"We needn't do that just now. They're as safe as if they were behind bars. There's something I want to do down here first—have a talk with Miss Tracy. She may be able to give us a little light."

"She can't help you," said Bassett. "They weren't on confidential terms. She'd be the last person he'd tell anything to."

He believed what he said, but his heart sank.

Anne to be dragged through another interrogation, an interrogation with a hideous suspicion behind it!

Rawson rose:

"Perhaps so, but it's worth trying. She may
know more than you think; sisters sometimes do.
And she certainly must have more knowledge of
him than any of us. We'll soon see."

He moved toward the door.

"I'll go up and get her now."

XV

WHEN Anne went up to her room she took a
seat by the window where she could see the channel. It was an undecipherable blackness, its farther limit defined by the shore lights. But the
night was very still, the sagging weight of cloud
hung low pressing down sounds. She could hear
the barking of dogs, the cries of children, a snatch
of song from the mainland. In this intense quiet
the first explosive throbs of a starting launch
would be carried clearly across the sounding
board of the water.

She kept telling herself that Rawson's absence
had nothing to do with Joe. She had been telling
herself the same thing ever since Williams' remark
at supper. She gave her reasons for thinking so,
as if she were trying to convince an adversary who
was maintaining an opposing position. It was as

Shine had said, Rawson had gone on some business they knew nothing of. There must be endless business connected with such a case. She remembered murder cases she had read of in the papers—accounts of false leads, trails picked up and dropped, legal questions of state and county authority.

Then across the water, running along the surface in stuttering reverberations, came the sound of the launch's engine starting. She saw the light leave the shore and come sliding forward, moving smoothly like a light held in a steady hand. Below it a golden dagger stabbed down into the glossy blackness of the current. She watched it approaching, the inside of her mouth like leather, her clenched hands wet.

When it had disappeared round the end of the house she faced the door and stood waiting. Her power to argue with herself was gone—if he had found out anything he might come for her. She calculated his movements: in the library now, talking with the others. A long time seemed to pass.

The stifling pulsations of her heart died down, and moving with an exquisite quietness as if any sound she made might bridge the space and call them running to surprise her guilty terror, she stole to the door and opened it a crack. The living-room was lighted but empty; they were in the library, shut in. Again a time passed and again her heart calmed to a slower beat. It must be business, the business that had nothing to do with Joe.

She closed the door and decided now she might rest, not go to bed yet, but lie down and try to get back to courage and control. She took off her dress and put on her negligée, and with hands raised to loosen her hair heard a step on the stairs. It struck upon her ear, heavy and quick, a man's step, and she remained as she was, her arms lifted, her eyes staring into her reflected eyes in the mirror. She stood thus till it stopped at her door. When the knock came and Rawson's voice spoke her name, the hands dropped and she moved to the door.

"Can you come down-stairs for a minute?" the voice said, low and guarded. "I'm sorry to ask you to get up."

She opened the door. "I hadn't gone to bed. Yes, of course I'll come. You want to——"

"Just ask you a few more questions. I'm glad I didn't wake you."

She followed him along the passage and down the stairs. They crossed the living-room side by side, Rawson with long strides, she with short quick steps. There was a sense of hurry in their progress as if they were hastening to some ominous goal. When she entered the library her glance fell on Bassett facing her across the room, his brows drawn low over the dark trouble of his eyes. His look told her of anxiety, apprehension and a passionate concern for her. She gave it back, feeling a desperate cold courage run to her fainting senses.

Williams indicated an armchair near the desk:

"Take a seat, Miss Tracy. Sorry we've had to call you down."

She fell into it and, as the men settled themselves in theirs, ran her tongue along her dry lips and took a deep breath of air into her lungs. Then she raised her chin and looked at them, inquiringly attentive. During the passage of the look she laid the charge on her mind to go cautiously and not be afraid.

"We've been making some inquiries about your brother, Miss Tracy," Rawson began. "About his leaving here. You told us, as I remember, that you knew he went."

"Why, yes, he went."

"Did you see him go?"

"Well, no, I didn't actually *see* him, but that wouldn't prevent—" She stopped and looked from one to the other of the watching faces— "What do you mean?"

She must find out what they knew before she ventured.

"Then you *didn't* see him?"

"No—I didn't see the boat go, I was up-stairs, but of course he went."

"We've found out that he didn't," said Rawson.

"Didn't go, didn't go back with Gabriel? Wh— why—" She swept them with an alarmed look which fetched up on Bassett. "Why, that's not possible!"

"Mr. Rawson's seen Gabriel." Bassett spoke very gently. "And he says he didn't take Joe over."

"But I don't understand. He was all ready. I said good-by to him."

"When was that?"

"In his room, just a little while before he went. He was waiting there, everything packed and ready, waiting for the boat."

"And he said nothing to you about changing his plans?"

"No, I don't believe he had changed his plans. It was his holiday, he'd been looking forward to it, he was crazy to go."

"Did he make any mention of an interview he'd had with Mr. Bassett?"

"No—I don't think he said a thing about Mr Bassett."

"And he told you he was going, wanted to go. Was he jolly and good-humored like a person starting on a holiday?"

"Yes—why shouldn't he be? It was what he'd been longing to do for years. After I left him I went to my room and dressed and when I went down-stairs I saw that his bag and fishing-rod, which he told me he'd left by the entrance, were gone, and I thought of course he was. And he has, he's gone some other way."

Bassett looked at Rawson and murmured:

"That's the explanation."

Rawson went on without noticing:

"Do you know of any adventures, schemes, he might have had in his head that would make him want to fool you, steal off without letting you know?"

"No, but I wouldn't. He didn't tell me much. Boys don't like their sisters interfering."

"When you saw him in his room did he say anything about Miss Saunders?"

"Miss Saunders? No—he was talking about his trip. But what are you asking me all these questions for? If he didn't go the way you thought what does it matter?"

"*You're* sure he's gone?" Rawson's emphasis on the pronoun was heavy.

She looked at him with startled eyes:

"Yes, aren't you? Why, you don't think he's *here?*"

It was evident that she had not grasped the sinister aspect of Joe's mysterious actions. It struck Bassett as odd, for he knew her intelligence and her anxious doubts of the boy. What she had been through, shock and lack of sleep, had blunted her perceptions. He prayed she would get through the interview without comprehending and he did not see how she could.

"How could he be here?" she went on, that look of naive astonishment fastened on Rawson. "What for? And if he was—if he'd missed the boat or changed his mind—wouldn't he be with us all, here among the rest of us? Of course he's gone—he's on his way to the woods now where he was going."

Rawson addressed Bassett:

"Didn't you tell me he was to stop to-night in Bangor and meet his friend?"

"Yes—they were to start out in the morning."

"Where were they staying?"

"Some hotel, I don't know the name. Do you remember it, Anne?"

She shook her head: "No. If he told me I've forgotten. I've no idea what it was."

"Hold on a minute," said Williams, stretching out his hand. "Shine spoke to me about that. He was asking about a hotel in Bangor young Tracy recommended—the Algonquin Inn. That may be it."

Rawson swung the desk chair round and drew the telephone to him:

"We can find out in a minute."

They sat without moving while Rawson made the connection. As he spoke the two men leaned forward, eagerly waiting, the girl drooped back in her chair, her hands in her lap, her glance on the floor.

"Is there a Mr. Tracy there—Joe Tracy?" And then a period of listening, punctuated with grunts of assent from Rawson. Then, "Mr. Travers has gone—left on the six-fifteen this evening—I see." A silent stretch and a final "Thanks—that's all I wanted. Much obliged." The receiver clicked into its hook, and Rawson swung the chair toward them:

"Travers has been there waiting since last night. Tracy never showed up. Travers had no message from him and left this evening for Moosehead Lake."

For a moment there was no comment. Anne raised her eyes, the sides of the room looked a long way off and the light seemed to have intensified to a violent glare as if she were sitting in the midst of a dazzling illumination. The men's faces were turned to her, glazed by the radiance like glistening masks.

"I don't know what to make of that," she said, the words dropping slowly with spaces between.

"Neither do we, Miss Tracy," said Rawson,

and leaning back, his hands clasped over his stomach, he gazed intently at her through his horn-rimmed glasses.

The glow increased, wrapped her round in a flame-like heat that ran along her skin in prickling points. It shone on the lenses of Rawson's glasses which seemed to grow larger and come nearer, malignly glaring.

"Yes, you do," she said and heard her voice hoarse and changed. "You've made something of it already. And what you've made is lies—wicked lies."

Then she had seen it. Bassett made a step forward, but she leaped to her feet, oblivious of him:

"You think he did it, just because you can't find him. That's all he's done, gone away. You must be crazy. What would he do it *for?* Don't you have to have a reason to commit murder?"

Williams was sorry for her, a pallid panting creature shaken out of her gentle semblance by an unexpected revelation. "Come now, Miss Tracy," he urged. "Don't get worked up."

But she paid no heed, pouring out her words at Rawson who remained without change of position, looking fixedly at her.

"They weren't good friends. I don't know why—I asked her but she wouldn't tell me. And what was it—a quarrel, a grievance? But that wouldn't make him want to *kill* her!"

"I've told them that, Anne," Bassett implored; "there's no use going over it."

She made a motion for him to keep silent and moved nearer Rawson.

"It *is* strange his going away like that—I'll admit it. But he did strange things; and does every one always do what's sensible and reasonable? Because he happened to act in a way that we can't understand is no proof he's a murderer. He didn't do it, he couldn't have done it. And to think that he's here! Where would he be? Haven't you searched the whole island? He's gone, even if he didn't meet Jimmy Travers. He's gone somewhere else."

Rawson leaned suddenly forward and caught her by the wrist:

"What did you see last night in the living-room?"

If he had meant to surprise her he failed of his purpose. She hung back from his grip and said with defiant emphasis:

"*I saw nothing!*"

"Are you sure it was a book you came down for?"

"It was a book, as I told you."

"You could read a few hours after your friend was murdered?"

"I could try to read—it was better than thinking."

"You've got a pretty cool head, Miss Tracy," he added, and relinquished her hand. She fell back in her chair as if his hold upon her had been all that sustained her in an upright position. He rose, looking down at her, curious and unsatisfied:

"I guess we'll call a halt for a while. We've other work to attend to. But wait here till we come back; we may have to do some more talking." He turned to Williams and gave a jerk of his head toward the hall. "Come on, we'll go up there now."

He walked to the door, Williams following him. As it shut after them Bassett went to her and bent over her chair. She held him off with a hand on his breast and whispered:

"Where are they going?"

"Up-stairs, to the top story."

She clutched the lapels of his coat:

"He's there, he's up there."

"He—who?"

"Joe!"

Bassett stared into her eyes. He thought her senses were giving way:

"Anne, darling, what's the matter? Joe's not here—you've just said so yourself."

"I said what wasn't true—he's there."

He caught her arms and drew her to her feet:

"What do you mean?"

"I know it, I've seen him."

"Seen Joe himself?"

"Last night when I came down for the book.

He's hiding up there—I thought he was safe.
And now they'll find him."

Bassett knew she was telling the truth. His
mind took a sweep backward over the last twenty-
four hours—she had known it all along, played a
desperate game single-handed. In flashes of ret-
rospect came her questions to him in the garden,
her ashen face when they had burst in upon her
the night before. The situation, accepted and
familiar, was suddenly shaken apart like the pat-
tern in a kaleidoscope and had fallen into another
shape, a shape so unexpected and horrible that he
stood frozen looking over her shoulder into its
unfolding dreadfulness.

"What can I do—what can I do?" Her whisper pierced to his brain and her hands jerked at
his coat in frantic urgency.

"Nothing now. They've gone, we can't stop
them. But tell me the rest—how did you know—
tell me everything."

"I saw the launch go without him and I was
going to speak to you, but Shine was there and I

couldn't. Then she was killed and I didn't know what to think, where he'd gone, anything! But that night I heard them say there was a man on guard at the causeway, and I came down to tell him in case he was here and would try to get across. And then I saw him."

"Where?"

"In the living-room. He came from the door into the kitchen wing and I whispered it."

"Did he say anything?"

"No—just ran the way he'd come in. And then I knew—" she stopped and closed her eyes. "Oh, I didn't know it but I thought it. *Can* it be true—could he have done it? One minute I'm sure and then I can't believe it; and I don't know, I don't know."

She pressed her face against his chest and he held her close, saying anything he could think of that might sustain her—they knew nothing yet—it was all guesswork—something might turn up that would explain it. He did not believe what he said—knowing more than she he had no doubts—

and under his words his thoughts searched wildly
for possible ways of coming to her aid.

"Oh, God grant it, God grant it!" she groaned,
and drawing away from him ran to the door, and
opening it, stood listening. He followed her and
with pauses for that tense listening, she told him
of her visit to the top floor.

"He didn't answer you?" he said. "Then he
might not have been there."

"Where else could he be?"

"Outside. He could see us going over the island
from one of those upper windows. After we'd
finished he could have slipped out again, knowing
he was safe there."

She saw the possibilities of this and hung on
them, left the door and conning them over, paced
about the room. Presently they could bear the
shut-in space no longer and crept through the
hall to the living-room. They stood on the threshold, subduing their breathing that no sound might
interfere with their entranced attention. The
silence of the house lay round them like an en-

shrouding essence. Far away the rhythm of the waves came and went, faint and regular, like the pulsing of the world's heart tranquilly beating in some infinitely remote realm of peace.

They returned to the library and, as the minutes passed and the strain increased, stood motionless and dumb as statues, waiting, listening. They felt as if everything but that room and their suspense had ceased to exist, as if time had stopped and this one fearful hour was to stretch out forever.

Then a sound from the distant reaches of the house broke it—the descending feet of the men. Bassett pulled her away from the door, closed it and drew her to the middle of the room.

"Will you help me?" she whispered. "Will you help me whatever happens?"

He nodded, there was no time now for words. He motioned her to sit down, and moved back from her, listening to the steps which were crossing the living-room, entering the hall. Were they louder than they had been going up, were

there three pair of feet where there had been two?
They stopped at the door, it opened and Rawson
and Williams entered.

Williams threw an electric torch on the desk
and said to Bassett with a sardonic grin:

"Nothing doing."

Rawson spoke to Anne:

"You can go up-stairs, Miss Tracy. We'll put
off the rest of our talk till to-morrow. You better try to get some rest. And kindly remember to
stay in your room. I don't want any mistakes
made about that to-night."

She murmured words of compliance and rising
with pale composure left the library.

When the door shut on her Bassett said: "You
got nothing up there at all?"

It had been difficult to frame the question.
Since they had left his position with regard to
them had undergone a horrible change. He did
not know how horrible till this first moment of
encounter when he saw them ready to meet him in
his old rôle. He felt a surge of repudiation and

then heard Anne's whisper at his ear. It drowned the call of his conscience, was louder than the guiding voices that had heretofore governed his life. She was fighting alone, she had begged his help and he was her lover.

"Not a thing," answered Rawson. "But we were at a disadvantage; not enough light, and it's a good-sized place. There's a big store-room full of junk, messed up with stuff, and one of the electric bulbs is broken. We couldn't go over that thoroughly, and he may have found a cache there. We'll comb it over to-morrow morning by daylight. Of course he could have got out on the island—all that kitchen wing's kept open. He might have been lying low up there all yesterday and have come down last night."

"And his sister saw him." Williams laughed with good-humored derision. "You didn't get anything out of her, Rawson."

"No, I didn't. She's either a very smart young lady, or an entirely innocent one. I'm not sure which. But she *did* lead us to believe he'd gone when he hadn't, she *did* come down-stairs on a pretty fishy errand, and she *did* forget the name of the hotel he'd gone to. All quite possible but—well, we'll know to-morrow." He walked to the window and looked out. "Dark as a pocket!" He turned to Bassett: "When the tide's full out could a person get across that channel except by the causeway?"

"There are places where they might swim the stream in the middle. It's a deep strong current but a good swimmer could do it."

"He might try it—he must be pretty keen about getting off here. You know this shore-line. Suppose you go down and take up a station below the boat-house among those juniper bushes. That's a place a person might use as a sheltered start for a get-away. You can't see but you can hear. Take Williams' gun, and if there's a sound, challenge, if there's no answer, shoot. I'll come down with you, I want to take a look at Patrick and I'll stay round myself for a while."

He stepped to the sill of the window but Williams, feeling for his revolver, stopped him:

"Hold on a minute. I got an idea that I think'll

help a bit. I've been thinking of it all day and if
I'm not mistaken it'll land your man or your
woman neater and easier than lying in wait for
them outside where they know by this time we've
got a guard."

Rawson turned back into the room:

"Let's hear it—we want to clear this up to-
night. But, Mr. Bassett, you go on. Stop and
tell Patrick what you're doing and see that he's
on the job. I'll be down with him later, unless
Williams' idea opens up something new."

Bassett took the revolver and stepped out of
the window.

The night was muffling dark; beyond the long
squares of light the windows cast, it lay a velvet
blackness, the murmurs of the falling tide issuing
from it as if it had a voice which was whispering
its secrets.

The outside darkness had a reflex on his own
soul. As his body moved forward into its shadow-
less density, his spirit sank deeper into an en-
shrouding gloom. He saw Anne in a circling
whirlpool, being sucked nearer and nearer to the

vortex. She knew Joe had never gone, had connived at his concealment, had lied to them at every turn—accessory after the fact. If they got the boy there was no way of extricating her and it was impossible that they should not get him, held here, all means of escape cut off. To-night, at the latest to-morrow, Joe would be haled before them. He thought of anything he could do, any wild act within the compass of human daring and ingenuity, and could find nothing.

He reached the boat-house and groped his way about it to find Patrick. Coming round the angle where the man was stationed he pronounced his name and was surprised to get no answer. He stretched a feeling hand which came in contact with a large warm bulk, immovable under his touch and giving forth a sound of heavy regular breathing. His own breathing stifled, his movements noiseless as a cat's, he struck a match and sheltering it with his curved hand, held it out. In its glow he saw Patrick huddled on the bench, his shoulders braced against the wall, his head drooped forward in profound sleep.

He dropped the match and put his foot on it. With the extinguishing of its tiny gleam the darkness closed blacker than before and he had to feel for the wall behind him, drawing close against it. The thought of his trust rose hazy in the hinterlands of his mind like the memory of some distant state of being in which he once had existed.

Pressed against the wall, he calculated the distances about him. The approach to the causeway was to his right, an incline of rocky steps, and in the stillness he could hear the lightest foot descending them. On such a night Joe might venture again—would venture if his nerve still held. If he did it would be within the next hour, and if Patrick slept and Rawson did not come he would go by unchallenged.

A fitful breeze arose, carrying sea odors. He saw the lights in the house go out, and the darkness close, solid and even, over where they had been. He heard the murmurings of the tide growing lower, fainter, till they sunk to silence and he knew the bed of the channel was uncovered.

XVI

WILLIAMS thought highly of his idea. It had come to him that morning while thinking of the person he had heard descending the stairs, the person he insisted was Mrs. Stokes. In its inception it had been directed chiefly at that lady, but now with the mystery complicated by the intrusion of a new figure its usefulness would be extended. The thing that was aimed at Mrs. Stokes, would include Joe Tracy. That was how he put it to Rawson to gain the consent and cooperation of his superior. For he had little interest in Joe Tracy himself, inclining to agree with Bassett and Anne that the boy had nothing to do with the murder and was not on the island.

It was a simple and practicable plan—a watch kept for the rest of the night on the stairs and certain points of exit. In the face of positive or-

ders two people had come from the upper floor
the night before, Miss Tracy on an errand that
Rawson thought suspicious, Mrs. Stokes, in Williams' opinion, to communicate with her husband.
Even if both men were wrong some powerful incentive was making them take such risks and it
was natural to suppose that incentive might be
strengthened after twenty-four hours of strain
and uncertainty. They might try it again, and to
catch them at it, surprise them in the act—if they
didn't break down on the spot—a little grilling
would do the job.

As for the boy—if he was still in the top story
as Rawson thought, he'd certainly not stay there
after they'd been searching the place for him.
He'd know they were on his trail, that his only
hope was getting away and the night was dark
enough to tempt him. If he was outside he'd
discover his escape was cut off and what would he
want then—food? He'd see himself faced by
starvation and the place he'd make for would be
the kitchen.

Rawson looked at his assistant with an approving eye. The idea was good, excellent, and without waste of time they arranged the distribution of the watch.

Williams would take the front stairs, his particular prey was there and he had already located the position of the electric-light button. Rawson would station himself in the kitchen with its two doors one to the outside, one to the hall. As Williams had pointed out it was the place to which Joe, escape blocked, would inevitably turn. The living-room they would assign to Shine, less important than either of the other ambushes, but commanding the entrance to the side wing and the path to the causeway and dock. Any one descending the back stairs to make an exit from the house would either turn to the kitchen or go through the living-room, and whichever way they took, would run into a trap. The men were satisfied, each one was detailed to the spot where he might expect to apprehend the object of his suspicion. The living-room, central and exposed, might safely be left to Shine.

They found Shine in the butler's room sleeping

soundly on the outside of the bed. He was acquainted with the plan, and stumbling and heavy-eyed followed them. In the hall Rawson left them, taking his way to his hiding-place, the other two faring on to the scene of Shine's duties. Here he received his instructions, special emphasis being laid on the door that led to the kitchen wing and the back stairs. Shine looked from the door to Williams with a perplexed frown. He did not like to admit—no more than he had liked to display the healthy vigor of his appetite—that he was so sleepy it was doubtful whether he could keep awake. In this embarrassing position, when he desired to acquit himself creditably and feared the weakness of his flesh, he too had an idea. He did not know if it would be acceptable and broached it with a cautious preamble.

They just wanted to know who the person was, didn't they? He wouldn't have to catch them, which would be nearly impossible in the dark and was unnecessary as no one could get off the island. To see them, be able to identify them, get on to

who was stealing round the house, was the point.
If that was enough he'd a way of doing it, the surest and most efficacious way it could be done, no
scrambling round the furniture, no uncertainty—
he'd set his small camera for a flash-light photograph. The materials were all at hand, he'd
gathered them together for a flash-light picture
of the company. All he had to do was to get them
ready and if any one entered by the door he was
to watch, he'd have their number before they
knew it.

Williams was interested—it was a neat trick
and tickled his fancy. As he was ignorant of the
process, Shine explained it, getting his properties
from the cabinet as he spoke. The flash-light
powder in a saucer on the table, then a double
wire extending from it to a point above the door—
the pair of antlers would answer. There the wire
would be cut, one-half hanging down from the
antlers, the other twisted round the door handle,
its end standing out. When the door was opened
the two severed ends would come in contact and

make the circuit which would set off the powder. He did not tell Williams that the taking of the picture could be achieved whether he was asleep or awake, but that the camera would make its record whatever his state was an immense relief to his mind.

Williams left and he quickly completed his preparations. The antlers served his purpose well, the depending cord was in exactly the right position and before he made his final adjustment of the two wires he unloosed the latch of the door that it might open easily and noiselessly at the first push of a stealthy hand. Then, his camera in place, he turned off the lights. The room was suddenly plunged into Egyptian blackness; he had to feel for the chair he had pulled up and grasping the tripod, nearly upset it. Swearing under his breath he found the arms of the chair and let himself down upon it carefully, to avoid creaking. The silence of the house closed round him, a silence that was like oblivion. The darkness showed no break as his glance traveled over it. A solid impenetrable wall, it was hard to look at, the eye required something to rest upon. After he had stared into it for what seemed a measureless stretch of time, he felt he must shut his eyes for a moment of respite. He did so, his head drooped, nodded, sunk, and he lay a big crumpled figure held in the embrace of the chair.

A bang—in that silence as loud as a cannon shot—a rending burst of light, waked him. He leaped to his feet his senses scattered, not knowing where he was or what had happened. Then from every side of the house noise broke, groans, screams, slamming of doors, thudding footfalls. It was terrifying in the darkness, like a company of ghosts wailing and running about in some black inferno. Williams' voice shouted the first intelligible words:

"You got them—good work! Where the hell are the lights?"

That shook Shine into consciousness, and he called to the gallery whence a patter of bare feet and shrill female cries rose:

"It's all right. Don't be scared. It's only a flash-light."

Male voices followed, harsh and loud as the men came rushing in:

Rawson's from the left with the crash of the door flung back against the wall.

"What are you doing in here? What was that?"

Bassett's from the entrance, his body colliding with furniture as he ran blindly forward. Somewhere in the darkness behind, Stokes' high and choked, breaking into curses. And over all Miss Pinkney's riding the tumult like the war cry of the Valkyries:

"Why don't some of you fools turn on the electricity? The button's on the right side of the door."

Bassett's hand found it and the room was flooded with light.

The women in straight white nightgowns stood on the gallery huddled together. The dreadful darkness lifted, they leaned over the railing, their

faces pallid between hanging locks of hair, dropping a shower of questions on the men below.
One of them was hysterical and gave forth a sob-
bing wail, and Williams shouted with angry
authority:

"Keep quiet up there. Nothing's the matter.
Didn't you hear it was a flash-light?"

Some one strangled a scream—Williams
thought it was Flora but could not be sure. Then
they made a simultaneous retreat to the bedrooms
for negligées and slippers, while the men, gathered
round Shine, listened to his explanation. No,
he'd seen nothing and heard nothing, but he'd got
the picture all right, whoever it was, he had them.
Now he'd go and develop it—he could do that in
a few minutes—and there was the projector in
the corner he could use, throw it on to something
where they'd all see. A sheet over that screen by
the desk would do. And when it's on there, large
as life, there won't be any use lying, there'll be
nothing for it but to come across.

They urged him out, they'd attend to everything: hurry up with the picture. Williams was unable to hide his elation. His idea, augmented by Shine's, was a bull's-eye hit, and his voice showed an exultant excitement as he called to Miss Pinkney to bring a sheet. Rawson's satisfaction was less apparent, but his eye was alight with anticipation. If it was the boy, he had run back up-stairs, for no exit had been attempted through the kitchen. With the whole house astir he'd be afraid to come down and they had him safe as a rat in a trap. Impatient at the wait for Shine's reappearance he left the room, saying he was going to the boat-house for a word with Patrick.

Bassett saw him go and made no move—he could not leave Anne now. The detonation and fire-work illumination that had made him leap for the path had roused Patrick. As he ran, not knowing what had taken place in the house, he had heard the man's grunt of returning consciousness and a hoarse expletive thrown into the night. Rawson would find him awake and his dereliction never be known. But this mattered nothing to

Bassett. An inner anguish held him; his eyes and
Anne's had met as she stood on the gallery and
for the despair in hers he had no consolation.
He saw Miss Pinkney and Williams pulling out
the screen and draping it with a sheet, he saw
Stokes walking stiffly to a chair, his hands curved
over its back, his face a curious shining white—he
saw and his mind registered nothing. If it was
Joe, if it was Joe—what would become of her,
what could he do?

The noise of the women's footsteps on the
stairs came in a descending rush. They burst in,
their voices going before them, a scattering of
gasped explosive utterances.

Flora went to Stokes and caught at his arm.
"What is it, what is it?" she kept repeating, jerking at his arm, till he started away from her pushing her off.

Williams heard and answered with veiled gusto.
Some one had been walking about the house at
night against orders. It had been important to
find out who was doing it and so Mr. Shine had

set his camera and caught them, him or her—Williams' voice was heavy on the last pronoun—in a flash-light picture. Mr. Shine was developing it now and as soon as he was ready they'd see it thrown on the sheet.

"It wasn't me," came Mrs. Cornell's voice in loud relief.

"Nor me, nor me." Flora's followed.

"Can't you damned women keep still," Stokes ground out between his teeth.

Rawson reentered. He had heard them as he came up the path and stopped on the threshold looking at Anne, waiting to see if she would speak. But she said nothing, standing by Bassett, her hand braced against a table, her glance on the floor. She knew Rawson was watching her and willed her form to an upright immobility, her face to a stony blankness. If she could hold herself this way, not move or speak, she could bear the tension. A touch, a word, and she felt that her body might break to pieces and her voice ascend in long-drawn screams to the skies.

The screen under its white covering was set in the place Shine had indicated, the projector put some distance back, facing it. To some of them these preparations had the hideous significance of those preceding an execution and all of them felt the deadly oppression of the approaching climax. The room was very still as if an enchantment lay on it. At intervals Mrs. Cornell drew her breath with a low moaning sound, Stokes' hands clenched and unclenched on the chair-back and Williams looked at his watch. He began a guttural mutter of impatience and stopped as the door opened and Shine came in.

He came quickly, bringing an air of excitement to the already highly charged atmosphere. There was a bewildered agitation in his face, and his words were broken and uncertain as he answered Williams' questions:

"Oh, yes, I got it—something—I can't quite make out—got me sort of flustered hurrying so. You'll have to stand away there, folks." He made a waving gesture and they drew back, pushing against one another till they stood massed in the rear of the room. He turned to the projector, adjusting it, then held the negative out toward Williams. "We'll probably lose this, Mr. Williams. Doing it so quickly I couldn't fix it. It'll likely melt with the heat in here, won't last more than a few minutes. You don't want to keep it, do you?"

"Go ahead. It's only the picture—that's all that concerns us."

"All right—it's your say-so. You'll get it in a minute now and by gum, I want to see—" he stopped, his breath caught, his hands busy over the machine. "Now then, we're ready. Some one please put out the lights."

Miss Pinkney pressed the button and the room dropped into darkness. Through it the projector cast a golden shaft that rested on the screen in a bright circle. The reflection painted their faces with a spectral glow. Every face, eyes staring, lips dropped agape or pressed together in a taut line, watched the bright disk of gold.

"Now," came Shine's voice whisperingly.

A picture leaped into being on the screen. A door-frame backed by solid indistinguishable black, the edge of a door, and beyond it, the outlines melting into the darkness, the suggestion of a head and shoulders only the face showing clear, looking at them with wide questioning eyes— Sybil Saunders' face.

The silence held for a moment, then broke in an explosive volume of sound. The women's shrieks rose simultaneously—"Sybil! Sybil!" The name ran about the room, beat on the high ceiling and was buffeted from wall to wall.

"The dead woman!" Williams shook Shine's arm in his incredulous amazement.

"It is—it's her. I saw it when I developed it and I don't know—something's gone wrong."

A raucous cry rose above the chorus of female voices. Stokes had dropped his hold on the chair, his starting eyes fixed on the picture. From his lips, curled back like an angry dog's, came a strangling rush of words:

"She's dead. She's dead for I killed her. I shot her—she's dead. She can't come back, she never can come back. I shot her as she ran—I killed her—I saw her fall—she's dead—dead!"

The words died in a groan. He pitched forward and lay a writhing moaning shape with hands that clawed and dug into the carpet. The men rushed at him, clustered about him, the women watching in dumb horror while the picture behind them slowly faded from the screen.

XVII

WHEN they carried Stokes to his room they thought him dying, so ghastly was his appearance, so deathlike his collapse. Bassett telephoned to Hayworth for a doctor and before the man came, Flora, singularly cold and collected now the fight was over, told them her husband was a morphia addict and showed them the case in his bag with the empty vial. In the two days' detention on the island his supply had been exhausted, the greatest strain of the many that had ended in his frantic confession.

When the doctor had made his examination and heard the facts he looked grave—the man was in desperate case, a complete breakdown of the whole organism and an overstrained heart. He thought there was little or no hope, but there might be a return to consciousness. If there was he promised to call the officers who were keen to

get a fuller statement. Meantime he wanted the
room cleared of everybody but Mrs. Stokes, and
the men left, returning to the living-room to find
Shine and get an explanation of the picture.

In the excitement of the Stokes sensation they
had forgotten all about the picture and now,
walking down the hall, they swung back to it.
Bassett and Williams were baffled and confounded by it; it was one of the most startling of
the whole chain of startling circumstances. Rawson was neither baffled nor confounded having
already arrived at a solution: Shine had played
a trick, done it on purpose to see if it might not
accomplish just what it had accomplished. He
was loud in his praise of the photographer, it was
a clever ruse that had brought things to a climax
when they might have gone on bungling for days.
Rawson was willing to admit his mistakes—he'd
been sure of the boy and now it appeared that
Bassett and Miss Tracy were right. Joe Tracy
had evidently lit out secretly on some business of
his own.

He dismissed the company with a curt command and as they made their hurried exits, jocularly congratulated Shine as the man who had pulled off a successful hoax. But the photographer showed no responsive pride, on the contrary he looked rather shamefaced and denied the charge. He'd meant to take a picture, no funny business or fooling about it—but—he rubbed his hand over his tousled hair and grinned sheepishly. He was sleepy, that's what had been the matter, just plain doped with sleep so he didn't know what he was doing.

"Well, how do you account for the picture?" said Rawson. "Are you one of these people who can take spirit photographs?"

Shine wasn't that—there was only one way of accounting for it. He hadn't opened the shutter and the picture was one of those he had taken of Miss Saunders the day of his arrival.

"Of course," he said, staring perplexedly at the carpet. "I'd swear I opened the shutter and I'd swear I closed it after I got my wits back. But there you are—you can't take a picture of a dead woman and I had a lot of her on that film. That's how it came about, being waked up sudden by Mr. Williams and trying to pretend I was on the job, and being naturally rattled by all that's transpired here. Oh, you can understand it!"

"You'd taken her like that—coming through a doorway?"

He'd taken two or three like that—he couldn't be sure how many. But he did remember posing her at both the front and rear entrances of the living-room, trying to get effects of a dark background with her figure dimly suggested and the light on her face. It was evidently one of those pictures, must have been the last he'd done, but he couldn't trust his memory on any small points. He'd been more shocked than he had any idea of but he knew it now.

He described his amazement at having seen it in the negative. He said he couldn't believe his eyes and hadn't mentioned it as he thought he was "seeing things" what with the murder and all the excitement. And he couldn't study it or compare it with those on the rest of the film because it was gone. After they'd taken Stokes away and he'd got the women quieted down he'd turned to the sheet—and there it was, blank as it is now and the negative melted. As for the explosion of the powder, that was easy to explain, and he told of his precautions in unlatching the door. Any light air could have swung it open and as he was sinking to sleep, he had felt a breeze blowing in from the entrance. Rawson verified this; a wind had arisen that had kept him on the *qui vive* in the kitchen, moving the curtains and making the doors creak.

So that was that! Nobody's brains, nobody's deductive powers, or perspicacity or psychological insight had brought them to the goal. The bungling of a sleepy man had done the trick.

They were talking it over when the sound of Flora's voice stopped them. She was standing in the doorway very white and very calm. Stokes was asking for them. Yes, she nodded in answer to Rawson's look, he was quite himself. The doctor had wanted him to wait till he was stronger but he had insisted:

"He says he must speak now while his mind is clear. He seems to know it won't last and he can't rest till he's told everything."

They found him bolstered up in bed, a haggard spectacle, his eyes, sunk in darkened hollows, seemed to hold all the life left in his body. They hung on the entering men, then swerved to his wife and he made a motion for her to sit beside him. When she had taken her place and he had groped for her hand, his eyelids dropped and he lay for a moment as if gathering strength.

"I'm glad you've come," he whispered. "Glad it's over. If I'm going on now it can't be to anything worse than this last thirty-six hours."

The desire to free his mind possessed him. Rest, he said, rest was all he wanted and it was not for him till he had unloaded the intolerable burden he had carried since Sybil Saunders' death. In his own words the recital was broken by digressions, memories of his torturing passion, assurances of good intentions that failed of execution, remorse for the wrong he had done his wife. Robbed of the theatrical quality that was of the man's essence, it was the stark revelation of a soul's tragedy.

He had never intended to kill her—that was the one point of exculpation he insisted on. His love had made him mad, carried him beyond the inhibiting forces of honor, feeling, reason. That it was hopeless seemed to increase its obsessing power, and she had never for one moment led him to think it was anything but hopeless. Unwaveringly, from the first, her attitude had been dislike, aversion, a horror of his state of mind and himself.

His knowledge of the coming separation had been the igniting motive that caused the inner explosion. After their stay on the island she would go her way, keep her whereabouts hidden from him, and he might never see her again. The thought became unbearable, and led him to a res-

olution of wild desperation—he would get her
alone, once more confess his passion, and if she
met it with the old scorn and abhorrence, kill
himself before her eyes. He had seen the revolver
in the drawer of the desk and on the day of the
performance, taken it. To prevail upon her to
grant him the interview was the problem, and the
evil inspiration came to him to tell her he had
news of Dallas, her lover. It was a lie, he knew
nothing of the man, but truth, decency, self-
respect no longer existed for him.

He described the interview in the living-room,
her roused interest and demand for the information. The intrusion of his wife worked with his
plan and he had insisted on a rendezvous where
they would be free from interruption. They
started for the summer-house on the Point, saw
Shine there, and made the arrangement to meet in
the place at seven. Then she had gone up-stairs
to her room and he to the balcony to wait for her.

When he saw her pass the balcony he had risen
and followed her. She had moved rapidly, not

waiting for him, and he had not tried to catch up with her as he knew she did not want any one to see them together. When he entered the summer-house she was sitting on the bench close to the table on which her elbows rested. His hysterical state, accelerated during the long wait, had reached a climax of distraction and he burst into a stream of words—he had lied to her, he knew nothing, but he had to see her, he had lured her there for a last interview, a final clearing up, and he drew out the pistol. The sight of it, his mad babble of disconnected sentences, evidently ter-rified her. She leaped to her feet and made a rush like a frightened animal for the opening. Before he could speak or catch her she had brushed past him and fled from the place.

Then something had gone wrong in his head— he couldn't explain—a breaking of some pressure, a stoppage of all mental processes. In the vacuum one fact stayed—that she had got away from him and he never would see her again. A blind fury seized him and he shot at her as she ran. She was at the summit of the cliff, staggered, threw up her arms and went over. When he saw her body lurch and topple forward the darkness lifted from his brain. He came back to himself as if from a period of unconsciousness and realized what he had done.

He described his state as curiously lucid and far-seeing. The insane outbreak seemed to have freed his intelligence and temporarily suspended the torment of his nerves. The situation presented itself with a vision-like clarity and all the forces of his mind and will sprang into action, combining to achieve his safety. From the shadow of the vines he looked at the house, saw Bassett come to the living-room entrance, glance about and go back. The sound of the shot had evidently roused no forebodings and when no face appeared at window or door, he ran to the pine grove. There he was safe and slipped unobserved to the balcony. He waited here for a moment to get his breath and compose his manner. He was the actor, playing a difficult part with a high-

keyed, heady confidence when he entered the
room.

His wife—that had been the unforeseen retribution. He had not realized that suspicion would
turn on her, and then saw that it might, saw that
it did. His hell began when he grasped the danger
she was in, listened to Rawson's questions on the
night of their arrival, sensed Williams' line of
thought when the scene was rehearsed on the
shore. He had tried to turn them to Joe Tracy,
snatching at anything to gain time, but he would
have told, he was ready to tell. He kept reiterating the words, his burning eyes moving from one
face to the other—he had broken her heart, ruined
her life, but he was not so utterly lost as that.

It was her assurances that quieted him. She
had known from the first he would tell as she had
known from the first he had done it. He relaxed
and sank back, his eyes closing, and the doctor
motioned them to go. Flora followed them to the
door and held them there a moment to repeat what
she had said—as if, like him, wanting to rid her

mind of all its secret agony. It wasn't surmise; she had seen him. When she had turned from the water after her attempt to catch the body she had had a clear view of him stealing through the pine wood, moving noiselessly and watching the house.

"He never knew it," she said. "That night when you, Mr. Williams, nearly caught me on the stairs, I was going to see him, say I knew what he'd done and that I'd help him and lie for him and stand by him. Oh, yes—I don't care what I tell now. He was my husband, I'd loved him and he'd been cursed—cursed and destroyed."

The men closed the door softly as upon the dead. What they had heard and left behind them had taken the zest from their accomplishment and in the glow of the hall lights their faces looked drawn and hollowed with fatigue. Rawson drew out his watch—half past two. The best thing they could do was to get a little sleep. The day would be on them in a few hours, there would be a lot of business to get through and he, for one, was dead beat. They wouldn't take off their clothes, just turn in on the sofa and divan, and stepping gently, as befitted a place where so dark a doom had fallen, he and Williams passed into the library.

Sleep was far from Bassett. He would like to have seen Anne, but it would have been inhuman to rouse her, and he went toward the living-room where he could think in quiet. The screen still covered by the sheet and the projector facing it were untouched and gave the place the air of a scene set for a play. Silence brooded over the room, a silence so peaceful and profound that it seemed as if the hideous tumult of the last hour must be a nightmare illusion. He dropped into a chair, his breath expelled with a groaning note, then heard Anne's voice from the gallery above:

"I've been waiting for you. May I come down?"

There she was, dressed, leaning against the railing.

"Come," he beckoned, his heart expanding, his depression lightened, and as she disappeared he pulled up a chair for her. She came in, soft-footed across the rugs, with the whispering words:

"I couldn't rest till I'd seen you and heard. He's told?"

"Everything." They sat, facing each other, close together. "It's solved and ended—the Gull Island murder."

"Is it all right for you to tell me?"

It was all right and he told her.

She listened absorbed, eyes intent on his, now and then nodding her head in confirmation of an agreement in her own mind. When he had finished, she sat looking down, apparently lost in musing contemplation of the story.

"So, as it turns out, Anne dearest, all that misery you and I went through was unnecessary."

"Yes," she said slowly. "It wasn't Joe, he wasn't in it at all. But I don't understand. I've been sitting in my room while you were with Stokes thinking about it and I can't make it out. Hugh"— she leaned forward and rested her hand on his knee, dropping her voice though no one was

there to hear—"this is what I can't explain—
whom did I see in here last night?"

Bassett's answer was prompt, delivered in the
brisk tone of common sense:

"I can. It's very simple. You didn't see anybody."

"Nobody?"

"Nobody. I've been thinking about it, too.
There's only one explanation, and that's it."

She looked beyond him at the lamp, her eyebrows drawn in a puzzled frown:

"You think I imagined it?"

"I know you did. Just consider:—You were in
a wrought-up condition, you expected to see him,
came down for that purpose. The room was almost dark, quite dark under the gallery where you
say he came from. After what you'd gone
through—first a murder, then a suspicion that
would have undermined the strongest nerves—you
were in a state to see anything."

She continued to stare at the light, her face
set in troubled thought.

"I suppose that could be."

"Why, Anne dear, it must have been, it could have happened to any one. And there's another point—if it had been Joe, wouldn't he have spoken to you, one question even to find out what was going on, what we were doing?"

"Yes, yes. I've thought of that. It didn't occur to me at the time. But he would have said something."

"Of course he would. You never saw anything more substantial than a shadow in the moonlight."

"That must be it," she murmured.

"I ought to have realized it but I was stampeded myself. We were all ready to go off like a pack of fire-crackers. God"— he took her hand and held its soft coldness against his forehead— "its a wonder we didn't all break to pieces like Stokes."

She was silent for a moment then said:

"Well, where *is* Joe? What's he doing?"

"Gone off on some business of his own. You were telling the truth when you told Rawson and

Williams that Joe's actions weren't always cal-
culable, weren't you?" He saw her answering
nod. "Well, he's evidently chosen the occasion
of his leaving the island to light out in some new
direction. You can't tell what may have been in
his head—a joke on Jimmy Travers, on us, any
sort of lark or tom-foolery. We'll find it all out
soon."

He had his own opinion of Joe's behavior which
he was not going to tell her now. The boy, found
out in his spying, knowing himself condemned by
his associates and black-listed in his profession,
might have departed for good, taken the opportunity to disappear from a part of the country
where closed doors and averted faces would be his
portion. It would be like him and Bassett fer-
vently hoped that it might be the case.

"Come," he said, rising and drawing her to her
feet. "There's no good bothering about that any
more. Leave it to me and when we've got through
the rest of this horrible business I'll look around
for him. And anyway, he'll see it in the papers,

and if he wants to show up, he'll do it himself within the next few days. Now you must go to bed and let your poor tired brain rest."

They walked to the door and there he caught her against his breast and looked into her face:

"It's all over—that fighting and struggling alone, Anne. After this we'll be together, as soon as we can get away from here and find a clergyman to marry us."

They kissed and parted, Bassett going to his room—he could sleep now—and Anne faring slowly up the stairs to hers.

XVIII

ANY one watching Gull Island from the shore
would have seen the yellow shape of one bright
window set like a small golden square in the darkness. The bright window was Anne's and over
against it Anne sat on the side of the bed looking
at the floor. She sat perfectly still, held in a
staring concentration of thought, reviewing the
happenings of the night. The inability to understand that she had expressed to Bassett had come
back to her, there were things that she could not
explain away. Like a child piecing together the
disconnected bits of a puzzle, she contemplated
separate facts, studied them, dropped each one in
turn and went on to another.

While Bassett had talked to her she had accepted his theory. His belief in it had been so
absolute and it was so plausible. Of course a per-

son in her state might have imagined anything.
And as she dwelt on the sentence to persuade
herself, the vision of the dim shadowy room rose
before her with the figure coming toward her from
the darkness of the gallery, moving spiritlike as
an hallucination might move. But as the memory
grew in vividness the shape took form and solidity,
the slim boy's shape. She saw again its rapid
advance, its sudden stoppage at her words, its
lightning-quick turn and soundless flight. The
snap of the closing door came to her mind as a
last confirmation and she knew it was no delusion.

"I did," she said in a whisper, and raised her
eyes as if confronting a doubter with the truth.
"I *know* it—I *did* see somebody."

Somebody!

The word struck her ear with a startling effect,
an effect of discovery, of impending disclosures.
Her body shrank together as if in fear of them,
her riveted glance grew fixed as a sleep-walker's.
She lost all sense of her surroundings, her entire
being contracted to a point of inner activity.

Before that intensified mental vision a series of
pictures passed like the slides in a magic lan-
tern:—Shine's photograph, the worn, wide-eyed
face of Sybil; Joe playing Sebastian, his costume,
his movements, a replica of Viola's; the living-
room' as they heard the shot, dusk falling outside;
in the summer-house—with its shrouding vines—
it would have been almost dark.

The pictures were disconnected like spots of
light breaking through darkness. If the darkness
could be dispelled and the spots of light joined,
fused into continuity, she would reach something,
something she was groping toward, fearfully
groping toward. Suddenly a recollection flashed
up, clairvoyantly distinct—Joe at the flat trying
to make Bassett give him the part of Sebastian,
imitating Sybil's walk. That picture brought
her to her feet, brought a smothered cry to her
lips. The spots of light had joined, run together
in a leaping illumination.

On the bureau lay the key of Joe's trunk that
she had brought from his room after their last

interview. She snatched it up and ran to the door, out of it, along the gallery. In Joe's room she turned on the light and unlocked his trunk. She went through it to the bottom looking for his Sebastian costume. It was gone, every appointment of it. She had not needed the proof, she knew that she would not find it, that it was Joe, dressed in that costume, Stokes had killed.

The rest of it—Sybil alive, hiding somewhere! She saw the gray dawn on the window—the night was over, the house would soon be stirring. She locked the trunk, turned off the light and stole out on the gallery. She did not go back to her room but kept on down the hall to the top-floor staircase. Half-way up she heard from the floor above a sound, so faint, so furtive, that it would only have been audible in the dead dawn hush. She made a rush upward sending her voice, low-keyed but passionately urgent, ahead of her:

"Sybil, Sybil, if it's you, wait. It's Anne. I'm coming to help you."

The door of the bedroom opposite the stair-

head was open. Against the pale light of the
window, poised with one hand resting on the
raised sash, was a boy's figure—surely the figure
she had seen in the living-room two nights before.
It was so completely boyish, the cropped round
head, the knickerbockers and belted jacket, that
she could not yet be sure and went forward with
slackened gait, peering and murmuring fearfully:

"Sybil, it *is* you?"

The figure left the window, came nearer,
silently, creepingly, with a hand raised for caution. She saw the face then, pinched and haggard, strangely altered with the curling frame of
hair clipped close, but still Sybil's.

It was so extraordinary—such a gulf of unknown happenings lay between them—that at
first they said nothing. In the spectral light they
were like two ghosts come together in some debat-
able land beyond earth's confines—too astonished
at their encounter to find speech, too removed
from the recognized and familiar to drop back to
its facile communications. They stared, eye to

eye, breath coming brokenly through parted lips, drawing together as if each were a magnet compelling the other. Anne spoke first.

"Joe," she said. "It's Joe that's dead."

"Yes. Do they know?"

"They know nothing. They think it was you. It's all over, Stokes has told. But, oh, what is it? I can't understand—it's like a fearful dream."

The words died away and a sudden violent trembling shook her. With the joints of her knees like water she sank on the side of the bed, gripping the other with her shaking hands, pulling her down beside her.

"Tell me, tell me," she implored. "Why is he dead? Why did he pretend he was you? What was he doing?"

They sat, clinging together, two small huddled figures in the gray light. Though the house below was as silent as the tomb they spoke in subdued voices, question, answer, surmise. Each knew a different aspect of the story, brought her own knowledge of Joe's motives and actions. In that whispered exchange they pieced together the separate facts, combined them in coherent sequence and came to a final enlightenment.

Joe had met his death in his last effort as a police spy, his last effort to get the Parkinson reward. Leaving his room to come down and make ready for his departure, he had heard the voices of Stokes and Sybil in the living-room. Sybil remembered Stokes' upward look and question about some one moving in the gallery—Joe creeping to concealment behind the arch. The nature of their conversation would have held him listening: here was his last opportunity to get the information he sought. He had heard the rendezvous in the summer-house. Its open situation offered no hiding-place outside, but knowing that it would be almost dark inside, he had conceived the idea of putting on his Sebastian costume and impersonating Sybil. He probably thought he risked no more than Stokes' rage, and he also probably thought that he might escape before Stokes had discovered his identity.

His room was next to Sybil's. He had heard her come up-stairs and from his window could command the Point. When Shine left it he had gone down, passed the balcony where Stokes was waiting, and hearing his following footsteps, moved with that close imitation of Sybil's gait to the summer-house. There the dim light and the drooping curls of his wig enabled him to carry through the deception. Stokes' wild speech, followed by the drawing of the pistol, had terrified him. Confronted by a man armed and half-mad, panic had seized him and he had made a rush from the place.

So Joe had died, a body clad in gala dress swirling out on currents that would never bring him back. Anne said nothing. She did not feel any special grief, or feeling of any kind. Too much had happened, she was benumbed. She had a vague sense that in some future time, when she had recovered from her dulled and battered state, she might be sorry, cry perhaps. Her eyes fell on her hand with Sybil's clasped around it and the sight of the linked fingers roused her. They were like a symbol of the intertwined closeness of their lives, so much closer than hers and Joe's had ever been. That brought her back to Sybil and Sybil's inexplicable actions. She lifted her head and looked at the face beside her:

"But—but—why did you do all this? Hide, not say anything, let them think you were dead?"

"I wanted to get away."

"Get away! What for—where?"

"To Jim Dallas. I know where he is."

"You've known?"

"For a month. I've written him telling him I'd come if I could, if I *ever* could. Oh, but it's been hopeless. I was spied on, dogged, followed—" Her voice rose on a hoarse note, stopped, and after a scared listening hush, went on whisperingly: "I want to stay dead, never come to life here again. It's my chance—the only chance I'll ever have. You've found me now and I'll tell you everything." And she told Anne the story—the story that no one else has ever heard.

Since she had received his address the longing
to join her lover had possessed her. She had
written she would come, she knew he was waiting
for her, but the watch kept upon her made any
move impossible. Whatever her anguish, she
could not risk betraying his whereabouts; if it
had been only herself she would have dared anything. In this position, growing daily more unbearable, had suddenly come the means of escape.
Tragedy, swift and terrible as a bolt from the
blue, had been her opportunity, and she had des-
perately seized it.

From her window, after the interview with
Stokes, she had seen Joe, in his Sebastian dress,
pass below. She had known it was he because of
the costume and was astonished, supposing him
already gone. Stokes came into view following
him and the disturbing idea seized her that he had
mistaken the boy for herself. She had run to the
door to go down and end the misapprehension,
and then stopped—at close quarters Stokes
would see who it was, and to let Joe—evil-tongued

and hostile—discover their rendezvous, was the last thing she wanted. She went back to the window to watch the outcome and saw neither of them. This frightened her—the only place they could have disappeared to was the summer-house. Stokes might say too much before he discovered his mistake, and panic-stricken, she was about to rush out, when Joe ran from the doorway and the shot followed.

For a space—she had no idea how long—she was paralyzed, not believing her senses. She remembered moving back into the room and from there she saw Stokes issue from the summer-house and flee to the shelter of the pine wood, *that* told her what she had seen was real, a murder had been committed under her eyes, and she went to the door to go down. Holding it open she paused on the threshold, heard the voices below, heard Stokes' entering words and had made a forward step to run down and denounce him, when a sound from outside stopped her. Flora's cry that Sybil was killed.

It was that wild screaming voice that gave her
the idea, sent it through her brain like a zigzag of
lightning. While the people below made their
clamorous rush from the house, she stood in the
doorway, motionless in contemplation of the possibilities that opened before her. The excitement
that had shaken her a few minutes earlier died,
her mind steadied and cleared, she felt herself
uplifted by an invincible daring and courage.
There was no danger of a recovery of the body
for she had heard from Gabriel and Miss Pinkney
that bodies carried out on the tide were never
found.

Alone on the second floor with little fear of interruption she had gone about her preparations
at once. She had taken nothing from her own
room but money from her purse (leaving a small
amount to avert suspicion) the candies from the
box on the table, a few crackers she had brought
up the night before from supper, and a pair of
scissors. Then going to Joe's room she had gathered the clothes he had discarded, lying ready to

her hand on the bed—everything from the shoes
to the cap—and stolen out and upward to the top
floor. Here she had put on the clothes and cut
off her hair—she showed Anne the ends of the
yellow curls in her jacket pocket—hiding her own
clothes in a box in the store-room.

As to when the police would be summoned and
of what their procedure would consist, she knew
nothing. Her hope was to escape by the causeway that night. From this Anne had saved her.
In her terror of recognition she had kept silent
knowing her voice would betray her.

The next day she had been a prey to a rising
tide of alarm. From behind a curtain she had
watched the search of the island and realized a
hunt through the top floor must follow. Every
sign of her presence was obliterated and she
studied her surroundings for a hiding-place. The
windows, opened half-way to air the rooms, suggested the possibility of a cache outside. Climbing up the wall and extending to the roof was the
great wisteria vine, its outspread branches twisted

into ropes and covered with a mantle of dense foliage. The main trunk passed close to the window of the room that faced the stair-head, the place where she sat waiting for ascending footsteps. When Anne had made her visit, she had heard the first creak of the stairs and crawled out under the raised window. With a foothold on the gutter she had slipped behind the curtain of the vine, her hands gripped round its limbs. Even from the garden below she thought it would have been impossible to detect her. Of Anne's whispered pleadings she had heard nothing; she had supposed the intruder one of the men. When they came up she had had plenty of time to hide for she had heard their footsteps when they came along the hall.

"Sleep!" she said, in answer to Anne's question. "I never thought of sleep. I was in this room all the time, waiting and listening. I didn't even dare to lie on the bed for fear I couldn't get it smooth again. The candies and crackers kept me from being hungry. But when your whole being is on such a strain you don't think of those things, you forget your body."

After the visit of Rawson and Williams she knew the danger of detection increased with every hour. Also the necessity for food could not be denied much longer. The one chance left her was to get away that night, make what she felt would be a last attempt to gain the freedom that meant life to her. The darkness was in her favor and she resolved to slip from the house and cross the bed of the channel below the causeway. She was a good swimmer and though the central stream was deep and swift she was ready to match her strength against it. If she failed—but she hadn't thought of failure—the goal to be reached was all she saw.

At the foot of the stairs she had hesitated, undecided whether to go by the living-room or the kitchen. Finally she chose the way she knew best, where she was familiar with the disposition of the furniture. As the flash-light burst she had made a noiseless rush for the stairs, was in the upper

passage when the women's doors flew open and
Rawson came running along the hall below. The
darkness and noise had covered her flight, but in
her eyrie on the top floor she had crouched at the
head of the stairs sick with uncertainty and
dread. The concerted shrieks of the women had
come eerily to her—cries of her own name. She
guessed then a picture had been taken, they had
seen it, and she waited not knowing what was coming. She had stayed there a long time, listening
with every sense alert, heard silence gathering
over the house and then gone back to her place by
the window:

"I hadn't given up, I had the spirit to fight
still. But it was so awful not knowing anything,
what they were doing, if they'd found out I was
alive. And what was I to do—stay here, get out
on the island? I couldn't tell, I was all in the
dark, and I felt my nerve weaken for the first
time. And then I heard your voice, Anne, 'I'm
coming to help you,' it said." She drew back and
looked with solemn meaning into the other's face.
"You meant it? You will help me?"

"Sybil, you know it."

"There's only one way you can."

"Any way."

"Let me go."

"Never tell—that you were here—that it wasn't you?"

"Yes, let me stay dead. Everybody believes it, let them go on believing. It *was* death, my life since that night when Jim disappeared. It wasn't worth going on with. Now I can go to him, be with him, there'll be no one watching Sybil Saunders any more. Even if I looked like myself it would be only the chance resemblance to a murdered woman. And do I look like myself?"

She turned her face to the light, bright now with the coming of the sun. Below the smooth sweep of hair across her forehead it was so changed in its pallor and thinness, so bereft of its rounded curves and delicate freshness that it was only a dim reflection of Sybil's—the face of a way-worn lad in whom the same blood ran.

The havoc worked by the suffering that had so transfigured it drove like a knife to Anne's heart.

She felt the prick of tears under her eyelids and lowered her head—Sybil gripping at her happiness with the fierce courage of despair, and now Sybil going, breaking all ties, going forever. For a moment she could not speak and the other, thinking her silence meant reluctance to agree, caught at her hands, pleading, with breathless urgence:

"They've accepted everything—it's all explained and ended. Joe has gone, dropped out of sight. Boys of his kind do that, do something they're ashamed of and disappear. What good would it do Stokes or Bassett or the police to know it was Joe who was killed? It's not lies, it's not being false to any one, it's only to keep silent and let me go. Oh, Anne, we've been real friends, we've loved each other— Love me enough to let me be happy."

The rim of the sun slipped above the distant sea line and sent a ray of brilliant light through the window. It touched their seated figures and lay rosy on Anne's face as she raised it.

"Go," she said softly. "Go. I'll never tell—I'll keep that promise as long as I live."

She could stay no longer, the house would be waking soon. There was a rapid interchange of last injunctions, information for Sybil's safety. To-night at low tide she would cross on the causeway. Every evidence of her occupation would be removed and with this in mind she took her Viola dress from its hiding-place and gave it to Anne. No one, ransacking the top floor at Gull Island would ever find a trace of her.

At the head of the stairs they clung together for a moment—a life-long good-by. There was no time for last words and they had no need of any. It was too solemn a farewell for speech. They were like shipwrecked comrades parted by tempest, Anne to find a haven, Sybil to ride forth on unknown seas, rapt and dauntless, following her star.

That night was cloudy—great black banks passing across the heavens. At times they broke and through serene open spaces the moon rode, silvering the sea, turning the pools and streamlets of the channel bed to a shining tracery. A boy's figure that had started across the causeway in the dark, was caught in one of these transitory gleams, a flitting shadow on the straight bright path. It stood out in sharp silhouette, running on the slippery stones, then clouds swept across the moon and in the darkness it gained the shore and the sheltering trees. Padding light-footed on the wayside grass, it skirted the edge of the village.

Dogs scented its passage and broke out barking; the sound following its progress till the houses were passed and the road stretched on between quiet fields to the railway.

Some people heard the dogs—light-sleeping villagers who turned and wondered if a tramp was about and lapsed into comfortable slumber. In the stillness of the room where Stokes lay unconscious, drawing toward the hour of deliverance, the barking sounded loud and insistent. The

nurse was disturbed by it and went to the window
and looked out, but Flora never heard it.   Anne
did and sat up in bed following it along the edge
of the village till it died on the outskirts.

EPILOGUE

THREE years later Bassett and Anne had a
friend at dinner. He was a writer who had just
returned from a successful lecture tour in Aus-
tralia. On his way back he had ranged through
the pleasant reaches of the South Seas and had
fallen under their spell—a little more money in his
pocket and for him it would be a plantation on
some isle of enchantment. Not the accessible
places, they were already spoiled, steamers had
come, jazz music, and tourists in pith helmets
with red guidebooks were under your feet. It was
the remoter islands, still out of the line of travel,
where a trading schooner was the sole link with
the world.

He had made a point of visiting some of these—
hired an old tub with a native crew and gone bat-
ting about and had a glimpse of the real thing
that Stevenson saw. And he enlarged on a par-

ticular island, the endmost of a scattered group, where he had found an American and his wife running a copra plantation. Delightful people called Whittier, he'd stayed several days with them in a long bamboo house on the edge of a lagoon—you couldn't imagine anything more beautiful.

Anne smiled at his enthusiasm and said she thought such a life might pall, especially on the lady. But he was convinced of the contrary, in fact Mrs. Whittier had told him she never wanted to come back, she couldn't stand the futile strain and bustle of the world. And it was not as if she were a person unused to the refinements of life, she was a pretty intelligent woman, cultivated and fond of the arts, especially the theater. She had asked him any amount of questions about plays and players—said it had been the thing she loved most in the old days. But she didn't regret it; she had told him she regretted nothing but the separation from her friends.

After dinner, moving about in the sitting-room,

the guest had stopped before a photograph standing on a side-table, picked it up and asked whose
it was. Bassett had answered—a friend of his
wife, now dead. But he would remember—it was
Sybil Saunders who had met with such a tragic
death some years ago. The guest nodded; of
course he remembered, a horrible affair. Then
after a last look at the photograph he turned to
Anne:

"It's like that Mrs. Whittier I was telling you
about. Just the same eyes—quite remarkably
like, only she's a bit stouter and more mature. It
might have been her picture when she was a girl."

When the evening was over Bassett escorted
the guest to the door. On his way back to the
sitting-room he thought he would suggest to
Anne that she put away the photograph—people
noticed it and the subject kept coming up. It
was evidently unbearably painful to her for she
rarely spoke of it; that dark chapter in her life
was a thing closed and sealed. He had the words
on his lips as he entered the room and then saw

that she held the picture in her hands and was looking intently at it, softly smiling, her expression tranquil, even happy. That was good—the wound had healed—so he said nothing.

THE END

Lightning Source UK Ltd.
Milton Keynes UK
UKHW050617041222
413305UK00029B/130